By Yi S. Ellis with Bryan D. Ellis

101 Stories for Foreigners
to Understand Chinese People

CHINA INTERCONTINENTAL PRESS

101 Stories for Foreigners to Understand Chinese People

by Yi S. Ellis with Bryan D. Ellis

First Edition © 2012 by China Intercontinental Press

Publisher: Jing Xiaomin

Editors: Wang Li, Haylie Chu

Illustrators: Zhang Yaoning, Liu Yanfeng, Luo Jie, and Pang Li

ISBN 978-7-5085-2414-6

Published by China Intercontinental Press

B-7 Shengchanli Building No.31 Beisanhuan Zhonglu, Haidian District, Beijing 100088, P.R. China

Distributed by China Intercontinental Press

B-7 Shengchanli Building No.31 Beisanhuan Zhonglu, Haidian District, Beijing 100088, P.R. China

Tel: (86) 10-82001477

Fax:(86) 10-82001477

http://www.cicc.org.cn

To my Grandfather, Chen Kun,

who reminded us to think beyond ourselves.

Author's Foreword

Let us introduce ourselves. My name is Yi Shen Ellis. I was born in Shanghai, emigrated to United States when I was thirteen, and spent most of my adult life in New York and Colorado. My husband Bryan D. Ellis and I moved to Shanghai in 2004 when he became the President of Bertelsmann DirectGroup in China. Three years into our China adventure, we wrote this book to share the hundreds of "cultural moments" and *faux pas* we encountered so that others can learn from them. Since its original publication in 2007, we have gotten feedback and suggestions from both readers in China and tourists from Australia, Europe and America. Five years later, we are happy to see that our book is still relevant in a fast-paced and constantly evolving China, and is now ready for this new edition.

We wrote our stories to illustrate how Chinese and Western people think, behave, and interact differently. These differences often cause misunderstandings. We've certainly made our share of cultural mistakes, and we'd like to share some of them so that you can avoid them too. During our years in China, we found it was not always easy living in a different country with a different culture. Too often, we slipped into the die-hard habits of judging another through our own cultural lenses. Doing so only builds "walls" and creates "us" versus "them". But when we learn the local customs and appreciate our differences, we open ourselves up to new ways of seeing the world. All of a sudden, many of the difficulties we encounter become much easier because we are able to better adapt to the local environment. This book, therefore, is our way of introducing the Chinese people and a small slice of their culture to you. It is the cultural "ABCs".

There are several clarifications we want to make about this book. First, we have written a collection of 101 anecdotes and cultural learnings to explain everyday Chinese customs and etiquette to foreigners. We are not scholars of Chinese culture, and this book is a decidedly informal and humorous one, not an academic discourse on modern Chinese culture!

Second, it is not a travel guide. Instead, it tells you how to interact socially and culturally with the Chinese people. We use stories to illustrate our learnings, *faux pas* and frustrations, and hope to give you a better understanding of and appreciation for the Chinese culture. Most of our cultural comparisons are between China and America, and the rest are between China and Western Europe, but we hope that readers from any country who is interested in visiting or working in China can benefit from these stories.

Third, you should not strictly apply the book's lessons to every place in China. China is a huge country, covering more than 30 provinces and encompassing 56 ethnicities. Each region of China has its unique dialect and cultural practices. While the stories in our book tell about the customs common to most parts of China, they are by no means comprehensive or exhaustive. In fact, quite a few of our stories are urban in nature because that is where we lived. So we urge you to keep an open mind and learn the local customs as you travel and work in various parts of China.

Last, the stories are written in Yi's voice, but it is a collaborative effort between both Yi and Bryan. Yi is the narrator because she had to explain

Chinese etiquette and customs to Bryan when they first arrived in China, and she's happy to do so for you as well. However, because of her bilingual and bicultural background, Yi is sometimes less sensitive to the cultural differences. This is where Bryan's accidental *faux pas*, moments of frustration, and puzzlement over certain customs provided the fodders for our stories.

Again, we want to thank Ms. Wu Wei from China's State Council Information Office who initiated and encouraged us to undertake this writing project in 2007. And many thanks to our publishing colleagues and personal friends who shared their stories, gave input, and saw this book from inception to this new edition.

We hope you enjoy our stories!

Yi S. Ellis with Bryan D. Ellis
December 2012, Santa Monica CA

CONTENTS

III. Restaurant Etiquette

IV. Everyday Etiquette and Customs

V. Beliefs

VI. Food and Drink

VII. Shopping and Gift-giving

VIII. Understanding the Chinese Family

XI. Raising Children in China

XII. Health and Medicine

I
First Encounters: Greetings in China

1. Happy to Hear "*Ni Hao!*" (Hello!)

Chinese is one of the most widely spoken languages in the world. More than 1.2 billion people speak it as their native tongue and it is fast becoming one of the world's dominant languages for business. However, it is a difficult language to learn, and so the Chinese people are very happy to hear any foreigner speaking it, no matter how little or how badly. My husband says that one of the most common phrases he hears in his daily life here is "You speak Chinese very well," and people often say this when he just says "*Ni hao*"(Hello)! It is a wonderful country in which to learn a new language, because whether you're talking with a taxi driver, a business colleague, a government official, or even ordering a coffee at Starbucks, the fact that you can speak even a little Chinese will immediately bring a smile to a Chinese face, and significantly more warmth to any conversation.

2. Shakes, Hugs and Kisses

When American men greet each other, they typically shake hands. When French women greet each other, they usually hug and kiss each other's cheeks. Most Western countries have a "shakes, hugs and kisses" culture, where people show their greetings and affections with their hands and lips.

In China, however, although shaking hands is becoming more common, people do not hug and kiss during greetings, even amongst good friends. A common greeting is a warm "Hello" and a nod, but nothing more physical than shaking hands, even among women. This is in keeping with the more modest and understated Chinese culture, whereby one shouldn't publicly show one's emotions and affections. It is rare for older Chinese husbands and wives to hold hands or show affection in public, and while the younger generation is becoming more liberal, the cultural modesty is still quite strong.

This sometimes causes some confusion with our friends from overseas, who tend to expect to hug our Chinese friends after sharing a dinner or evening out. Most of our Chinese friends now expect such affection from Westerners, and are happy to respond in kind, but not with their own Chinese friends!

3. Mrs. Wang's Husband Is Not Mr. Wang

A good friend of mine is a very successful Chinese business woman working for an American firm. On a visit to China, her American boss invited my friend and her husband to dinner. My friend's last name is Wang, so when the American boss met her husband, he shook his hand warmly and said, "Ah, you must be Mr. Wang. It's so good to meet you." My friend's husband replied, "It's nice to meet you, too. But actually, I am not Mr. Wang, I am Mr. Liu."

In mainland China, almost every Chinese woman marrying a Chinese husband keeps her maiden name after marriage. This has been the custom since 1949 when the Chinese Communist Party began to rule the country. Under communism, women and men are supposed to be equal. In fact, a popular slogan in the 1950s says that "Women hold up half of the sky." Maintaining one's maiden name is also a sign of women's independence from men. Today, it is less a political or social statement than it is a habit. I know no mainland Chinese woman who changed her surname after marriage. In contrast, most

Chinese women in Hong Kong and in Taiwan will add their husband's surname to their own so that their names begin with two surnames.

So next time you meet a Chinese couple in China, remember that Mrs. Wang's husband is not Mr. Wang!

4. Firm or Soft Handshake?

For a long time, Bryan wasn't sure whether one of his joint venture partners liked him because he never returned Bryan's firm handshakes with any vigor or conviction. The exchange was always brief as if he didn't really care to shake Bryan's hand. Over the past few years, the two of them have enjoyed many dinners, drinks and meetings together. All other indications show Bryan that they have a good relationship with each other, so Bryan has simply ignored his weak handshake as a cultural difference.

Indeed, after a few conversations with several Chinese friends, both men and women, I realized that there is a big cultural difference regarding handshakes.

In the West, a firm handshake is a sign of confidence and sincerity. Aware of this, most men and women in Europe and America shake hands with a solid grasp and a strong squeeze.

In China, the handshake culture is quite different. Although many Western-educated Chinese or Chinese business men and women who frequently work with foreigners also have firm handshakes, most others do not. Bryan and I have often found that many Chinese have a very soft or weak handshake. For most

Chinese, a handshake is not a way to show one's confidence or sincerity. Instead, it is just a formality that people have to go through, sometimes even with reservations.

I think that deep down, many Chinese are uncomfortable having intentional physical contact with strangers (I add intentional here because people are not bothered by bumping into each other on crowded streets). Even among the Chinese, handshakes between strangers are perfunctory. This discomfort is compounded when the handshake is between a Chinese and a foreigner. A decade

or a two earlier, most Chinese had not even seen any foreigners on the streets, much less shaken hands with them. Now, even though there are many *laowais* (a Chinese nickname for foreigners which literally means good-old-foreigner) living in China, having direct physical contact with one is still the exception rather than the norm. Therefore, most Chinese are a bit shy when they have to shake a *laowai*'s hand.

Among friends, the Chinese do not usually use a handshake as a way of greeting. Between men they typically pat each other on the shoulder to say "hello" and express familiarity. Between women, they usually hold each other hands or touch each other's forearms to indicate close friendship. The only time one witnesses a vigorous handshake between two Chinese is when two really good friends, typically men, have not seen each other for a long time. The enthusiastic handshake is a way of saying, "Long time no see! I've really missed you!" Between two long separated girlfriends, the Chinese prefer to hug each other instead.

A handshake between a male and a female is especially tricky. I find that when I shake hands with another Chinese woman, the grasp is often firm and without reservation. But when I try to extend a firm shake with a Chinese man, the reaction I meet is typically the opposite from what I would expect with a Western man. With a Western man, my firm shake would be met with an equally if not harder squeeze back. But in China, the harder I try to squeeze, the weaker the reaction. It is as if they are put off by my firmness.

It turns out that it isn't just with me that Chinese men do not shake hands firmly; they don't do it with any woman, especially not with any young Chinese ladies. Almost every Chinese man I interviewed told me that they do not want to squeeze a woman's hand hard because they don't want to appear rude. Shaking a woman's hand firmly may be mistaken for being too eager. Holding her hand too tightly might be seen as harassment. In order to avoid these potential misunderstandings, the Chinese men choose to err on the safe side. A weak handshake is much better than being accused of forwardness or impropriety.

Likewise an unmarried Chinese girl is likely to have a very soft handshake with a man because she does not want to appear too forward. Prior to the 20th century, Chinese women did not have any physical contact with men other than those in their immediate family. She was not even allowed to see or touch her betrothed until their wedding night. Although this is no longer the case today, many unmarried Chinese women still keep a physical distance from men outside of their family. When they have to shake hands, they do it ever so lightly to maintain their "untouchable purity." Shaking hands firmly would be too aggressive and too unladylike.

So when you shake hands with a Chinese person, don't presume they lack confidence or sincerity just because they don't have a firm handshake. Just remember that the handshake culture in China is quite different from that in the West.

5. Where Are You From?

I was recently at a business dinner with both Europeans and Chinese guests attending. One European guest asked a Chinese guest, "Where are you from?" The Chinese guest looked at me and asked, "Does he want the Western answer or the Chinese answer?"

When Westerners ask, "Where are you from?" they mean "Where were you born?" and "Where were you raised?" But when a Chinese asks another Chinese, "Where are you from?" it typically means "Where is your father's ancestral home?"

This can often be confusing because a person can be born and raised in a completely different place from their ancestral home town. For example, one of Bryan's colleagues was born and raised near Nanjing (a few hours train ride from Shanghai), but his ancestors are from Guangdong province in the south of China. So when the Chinese asked him where he is from, he answers, "Guangdong," and immediately people assume that his native tongue is Cantonese. But in truth, he has never lived in Guangdong and cannot speak Cantonese at all.

Similarly, both of my parents' families have lived in Shanghai for at least three generations. But when asked where they are from, they refer to their respective ancestral homes. Thus, despite being born and raised in Shanghai, having spent two thirds of my life in the United States and having an American passport, I am still expected to say that I am from Ningbo, a town which I have never seen.

6. You Are One When You Are Born

The Chinese calculate age differently than Westerners do. They believe that when you are born, you cannot be zero years old, so at birth, you are already one. Then, after the Chinese New Year, you add another year! So if you are born in the second half of the year according to the solar calendar, your Chinese age would be two years older than your actual age.

For example, our son was born in December. In the Chinese tradition, he was one when he was born. But in February, after the Chinese New Year arrived, he was already two, even though he was barely two months old.

This system is often confusing, even for our Chinese friends, so people typically just ask what your Chinese zodiac sign is and use it to calculate your age. There are twelve zodiac signs, each lasting one year before the whole cycle repeats again. When someone tells you their zodiac sign, you can quickly figure out, based on his approximate age, what year he was born and how old he is. It is also a polite way to find out someone's age without asking it directly.

The twelve Chinese zodiac signs are: rat, ox, tiger, rabbit, dragon, snake, horse, goat, monkey, rooster, dog, and pig. People commonly associate each sign with a specific personality. Rat likes to snack; ox works hard; tiger is passionate; rabbit is sensitive; dragon is powerful; snake is the lesser dragon; horse is righteous; goat is a lucky sign for men; monkey is clever; rooster is proud; dog is loyal; and pig is the luckiest sign of all.

II
Chinese Modesty

7. Virtue of Modesty

A couple years ago, Bryan and I went to Beijing to visit my extended relatives (my maternal great-grandmother had 12 children, so I have a lot of grand aunts and uncles!) We had a big family reunion in Beijing, and during dinner, everyone took turns talking to Bryan and testing his Chinese. They were pleasantly surprised by how well Bryan can communicate in Chinese, but when they complimented him on his language skills, they quickly saw that he didn't fully understand Chinese culture. When one aunt said "Your Chinese is very good," Bryan responded like a true American and said, "Thank you." She immediately corrected him by saying that he should have responded, "No, it is not, I still have much to improve upon!"

Thanks.

You'd bettet say "No, I'm not good enough yet."

8. Can't Take a Compliment

Many Chinese people are embarrassed by compliments, and when complimented, they quickly deflect it by playing it down. This is part of the modesty that governs Chinese social behavior and makes Chinese people appear much more humble than most Westerners.

For example, I saw an acquaintance one day and complimented her on her great new haircut and outfit. Instead of saying "thank you" she immediately replied, "No, I don't look nearly as young and pretty as you do." At first I thought that that was a strange way to answer a compliment. But later I began to see that kind of exchange among almost all Chinese women and I began to understand why. It was a way to show their embarrassment and to give a compliment back to their friend.

Many Chinese people are acutely aware of the differences between how Westerners and Chinese receive compliments. In fact, it is somewhat of a joke now how Bryan and I react to compliments paid to us by Chinese friends. While writing this book, the Vice Director General from the State Council Information Office met with Bryan and me to inquire about the progress of the writing. Upon meeting me, she said to Bryan, "Your wife is quite beautiful." He answered,

"Thank you" in Chinese. She commented "That was quite an American answer."

"The Chinese" she added, "would say '*Na li, na li* '" which literally translates to

"Where, where?" but really means "No, not really."

9. Humility vs. Confidence

One day I was having lunch in the common kitchen of an art studio where I take painting lessons. I overheard a conversation between a Chinese lady and a teenage girl who had been educated at a Shanghai International school. The older lady was preparing a traditional Shanghaiese dish for lunch.

Girl: *What are you making?*

Lady: *Oh, I am making a cold appetizer with tofu.*

Girl: *Aren't you going to cook it?*

Lady: *No, you can eat tofu cold too.*

Girl: *Does it taste good?*

Lady: *I think it should taste OK.*

Girl: *What do you mean "should"?*

Lady: *Well, not everyone likes the same things. One thing may taste good to one person, but may not taste good to others.*

Girl: *But you made it, didn't you?*

Lady: *Yes...(She was a little puzzled.)*

Girl: *Well, then you should say "It tastes quite good!" You should have confidence in your own creation!*

At that, I broke out in laughter. In defense of the Chinese lady, I said,

"Well, you see, a Chinese person would never say that about their own creations. It would sound too cocky. She was being modest when she said 'It should taste OK.'"

To that, the girl replied, "I still think she should say, 'I think it tastes good!'"

Although most Chinese are uncomfortable not being modest, a new generation of young adults in big Chinese cities are becoming increasingly more "confident," and therefore "less Chinese" in that way. Many youngsters now say "thank you" when complimented, and they have no trouble showing how proud they are of their work! The Chinese lady at the painting studio commented that "These kids are becoming more and more Westernized."

10. Don't Show Off, Especially Your Wealth

In America, people say "the squeaky wheel gets the grease," but in China, they say "the nail that sticks out gets hammered down." Even though the gap between the rich and the poor has widened in China in the past decade, the appearance of social equality is still important.

I have a Chinese friend whose husband is a very successful entrepreneur. He loves cars so he bought a Mercedes and a BMW. However, he almost never drives them. He continues to commute to work in an old black Buick. Now that they have two children, I thought they would buy a fancy Mercedes minivan, but instead, they bought a local Chinese-made brand with minimum trappings. When I asked my friend why they didn't buy what they could easily afford, she replied that they don't want to appear too wealthy. It attracts too much attention, and they want to avoid envy and jealousy from their employees and friends.

11. "I Will Do My Best"

Chinese cultural modesty is reflected in the work world. My husband was initially surprised by one specific difference in how people answer the question, "Will you achieve your targets?"

In America, when my husband asked his staff, "Will you achieve your targets?" they would either respond "Yes, we will", or "No, we will not unless we make the following changes..." This answer showed my husband that his people had confidence in themselves and their capabilities, and that if they didn't feel they would meet a goal, they would be blunt in saying "no" and asking for his help to turn this into a "yes."

In China, however, people frequently answer this question with, "I will do my best." He hears it when talking about budgets; about fixing a broken air conditioner in the office; about implementing new IT systems; and in many other instances. And this seems reasonable because, after all, what more can one ask than for people to do their best?

However, to Western ears, this sounds like they are not confident in themselves, or that they are unwilling to commit themselves to their targets. Bryan said that this answer made him nervous because he couldn't tell if they were just being modest, if they really didn't think they could do what he wanted, or if they wanted an excuse if things didn't work out ("I never said I could...").

So Bryan now answers, "OK, thank you for doing your best. Will doing your best achieve the target?" And he won't stop until he gets an answer, either yes or no, and it really seems to work!

12. Thin Face and Thick Skin

When my husband started working in China, he spent a lot of time speaking with his new senior team to get to know them, and better understand how he should manage them. He quickly concluded that he would respect his Chinese staff members' culture, but would also introduce some New York-style management to his team. One key area was "face," or honor, which is very different in China than in the Big Apple.

In China, "face" is extremely important, and any slights or criticisms that offend someone's honor are taken personally. When Chinese people say someone has a "thin face," it means that this person is easily offended by criticism. Accordingly, Bryan found it difficult to have staff meetings with his team because his staff would not openly discuss their opinions or challenge other people's ideas. People would speak openly during private conversations but not in group discussions. While this was respectful for people's feelings, Bryan found that it made management change very difficult.

So Bryan told his team about "face" in New York, saying, "In New York City, you have to be able to take criticism, challenges and suggestions without letting it get to you, and to keep smiling. We call this having 'Thick skin!'" Now Bryan's team is able to have open discussions about company strategy and sensitive issues, combining their respect for each other with a bit of "thick skin."

III
Restaurant Etiquette

13. The Chinese Seating Chart

Seating location holds very different importance in China than in most Western countries. In fact, great care must be taken to seat people properly to avoid offending anyone.

In Western countries, people usually don't attach a lot of meaning to seating arrangements. During business meals and when friends get together in restaurants, guests often choose where they would like to sit. When the meal is served at someone's home, such as Christmas and Thanksgiving dinners, the hosts typically sit at the two ends of a rectangular table, and the guests are seated along the long sides. Guests are often arranged so the pattern is man, woman, man, woman, but otherwise not much meaning is attached to who sits where.

In China, the tables are usually round and seat ten at a time. The seating position corresponds to a person's importance rather than to gender. The person sitting farthest from the entrance is the guest of honor. This seat is reserved for the most senior person according to social hierarchy. The person closest to the door, usually opposite the guest of honor, is the person who will be paying the check. That person is not necessarily the main host. For example, he could be the assistant to the main host who will take care of the bill. Everyone else around the table is seated according to rank. People close to the guest of honor are ranked higher; people close to the door are ranked lower.

There is usually a turn-table, or "lazy Susan," in the middle of the table to make sharing of dishes easier. The waiters will always place an entrée immediately in front of the guest of honor. Only after he/she has taken a serving will the junior person turn the turn-table to serve the others.

14. Private Rooms at Restaurants

My husband is an extrovert, so he likes to go out and see people. Even when it's just the two of us going out to dinner, he likes to go to crowded restaurants where there is good atmosphere. So he was very surprised by his restaurant dining experiences in China, because when people go out to eat here, they often eat in a private room.

When we arrived in China, my extended family welcomed us by taking us out to eat. We had spent the first several days having dinner with my parents and grandmother at their homes, so Bryan said that he was excited to go out to eat and sit in the middle of a restaurant surrounded by the bustle of other diners. However, when we arrived at the restaurant, the maitre'd showed us to a private room that had a big round table, a sofa, and ten chairs in which to seat all our relatives. The room had its own waiter, stereo system, and even had its own restroom! So when my parents, grandmother, aunts and uncles all filed in, Bryan leaned over and said "I thought we went to a restaurant to go out, but it feels like we went to a restaurant to eat at home!"

I explained to him that it is very common in China for families and groups of people to eat in private rooms, so that they are not bothered by other diners and can visit with each other easily.

15. Shouting for Waiters

The first time Bryan and I went to a bustling Chinese restaurant with a good Chinese friend, we were taken aback by how loudly he shouted at the waiters to get their attention. This particular friend was educated abroad and was normally soft spoken, so it seemed quite out of character for him to shout so loudly at anyone.

As we go to more Chinese restaurants, however, we find that at inexpensive to mid-range restaurants, shouting for a waiter or a waitress is more the norm than the exception. In fact, if you just raise your hand or call out quietly, you could be ignored for a very long time, as the waiters and waitresses at these huge and busy restaurants will not notice you at all unless you shout.

At first, Bryan and I were self-conscious and restrained about calling loudly. However, after a few futile attempts, we started calling "waiter" (*fu wu yuan*) quite loudly. Immediately, a waiter appeared and as we looked around guiltily, we saw that no other patrons had turned their heads to stare at us or disapprove of our "rude" behavior. Now Bryan confidently shouts for waiters' attention in busy Chinese restaurants but he always explains the custom to our Western friends first so that they do not wonder why he is being so impolite.

Explanatory Note:

Shouting for waiters is not necessary in every restaurant in China. You don't need to, and should not, call out in quiet restaurants and in expensive Western-style restaurants. In those places, the waiters are usually in closer proximity and are able to see your raised hand.

16. One Menu per Table

In most countries we have visited, we are offered one menu per person at restaurants. Each person then picks what he or she wants to eat. Dishes are typically not meant for sharing.

In China, most restaurants, especially if they serve Chinese cuisine, will offer you only one menu per table (If you have ten people dining, they may give you two menus). Chinese restaurants expect that one person will do all the food ordering for everyone at the same table. (Drink orders are taken individually to suit each customer's needs.) All dishes are meant to be shared among many people. In fact, we often find it very difficult to order at a Chinese restaurant in China when there are only the two of us. The portions are usually too large if you want to order a variety of dishes. You would need at least four people to strike a balance between the size and the variety of the dishes.

We had a couple of friends visiting China from New York City. They went to lunch at a Chinese restaurant by themselves. After sitting down, they asked their waiter for an additional menu so that they would each have one to browse. For them, it was perfectly normal to see the menus individually and decide what to order. But to the Chinese waiters, their asking for an additional menu meant something was wrong with the service. They are simply not used to guests asking for more than one menu when there are only two people eating!

17. Where Are My Appetizers?

When we have friends from the United States visiting us in China, we always try to take them to Chinese restaurants for an authentic experience.

One time a friend requested pot-stickers, or pan-fried dumplings, and wonton soup because those were her favorites. So I made sure to order these two foods with the rest of our order. Having walked around Shanghai all day, our friend waited eagerly for her food. But when the dishes came, she noticed that her favorites were not among them. Instead, there were only a few dishes of cold appetizers. When they started bringing out the main entrées, she leaned toward me and asked, "Where are my appetizers?"

Only then did I realize that I had forgotten to tell the waiters to serve the dumplings and the wonton soup first. In Chinese restaurants abroad, both pan-fried dumplings and wonton soup are considered appetizers and are served before the main entrées. But in China, soups and all forms of carbohydrates are served last. People eat them after all the main courses are finished. Our friend would have had to wait all night for her "appetizers" if I hadn't made a special request for them to be brought out early!

Similarly, Bryan was used to having rice with his main entrée in Chinese restaurants in the United States. When we first arrived in China, we noticed that rice would come after we were almost done with our meal. Most Chinese, in fact, don't even eat any rice in restaurants. So we learned that if we wanted rice with our meal, we had to ask the waiters to bring it out with the entrées.

18. Seat Covers in Restaurants

When we had just moved to China, we went to dinner at a Peking duck restaurant in Shanghai. Bryan was wearing a sport coat and I had a wrap, both of which we hung on the back of our chairs when we sat down to eat. We were quite surprised when the waitress immediately took a brown cloth sack and pulled it over the backs of our chairs, covering the coat and wrap completely.

It was obvious that the cloth sack was a seat cover, but we wondered why we would need covers in this particular restaurant. As we ate in more restaurants, however, we saw that many restaurants will cover their patrons' chairs and then we realized why. Chinese food features many soups, sauces, spices, teas and other liquids. These could easily stain clothing if a waiter carrying them is bumped or jostled and many Chinese restaurants put their tables so close together that this can easily happen. Chinese restaurants also permit smoking, so the sack helps keep the odor of cigarettes off the jackets and wraps.

One other benefit for women is that the cloth sack can also cover a purse or bag. When I lived in New York, I had the awful experience of having someone steal my purse while I was at a restaurant eating dinner. I had hung my purse on the back of a chair right between my husband and me, and yet someone managed to steal it right in front of our eyes. I really appreciate the fact that my bag can be safely covered up and protected so that no one can steal it while I'm eating or in the restroom.

19. Toasting

In Europe and North America, people typically toast once at the beginning of a meal, and maybe once in the middle if someone wants to make a speech. But in China, people toast throughout the meal and do so in a very specific way.

At the start of a meal, everyone joins in for a group toast. Afterwards, during the meal, various people will make individual toasts with specific people; the highest-ranking people will toast each other, the junior staff will toast their superiors, the host will toast the guest of honor, and so forth. Some toasts are for the whole table, but many toasts are just one-on-one.

The amount people drink for each toast will also vary, with some toasts finished with a small sip and others requiring the participants to empty their glasses (called *ganbei*). Generally speaking, emptying one's own glass is a sign of respect and sincerity toward one's drinking partner. A person with a higher social rank should drink less than someone with a lower rank. For example, when a junior staff drinks with a senior person, the junior staff will usually empty his/her glass, while the senior person will take just a sip. Senior people drinking together can either sip or *ganbei*, while the host will usually have at least one *ganbei* with the guest of honor to show sincerity and strong friendship. Similarly, junior members of two different departments or companies will *ganbei* when toasting each other to cement their relationship.

The toasting phrase is also different depending on whether you empty the glass or just take a sip. If you want to ask your partner to finish the glass, you say "*ganbei*" for "bottom's up." Once you have downed the drink, you tip the

glass over to show that there is nothing left. If you want to do a mild toast where everyone can just take a sip, then you say "*suiyi*" which means "as you like."

You also need to know how to clink your glass. One of Bryan's helpful Chinese joint venture partners taught us this etiquette. When you toast someone who is more senior in position, then you want to lower your glass so that when the glasses meet yours is at a slightly lower position than his. If you are toasting someone who is your equal, then you clink your glasses at the same level. If your subordinates are toasting you, then your glass should remain a little higher than his.

Sometimes, to pay extra respect, the Chinese will intentionally lower his glass in relation to yours even if he is your equal. In that case, you have to lower yours to match his. That often disintegrates into a competition to the extent that both glasses hit the table and reach a point where they will go no lower. When individuals are toasting as a big group around a big table, everyone will tap his glass on the round glass in the middle of the table as a substitute for physically clinking the glasses.

20. Slurping Hot Soup

Both Bryan and I love eating hot Chinese breakfasts at the food stalls in the narrow streets of Shanghai. They serve delicious noodles, wonton soups, buns and pancakes. Despite his appreciation for these culinary delights, however, Bryan has found it impossible to stand the noise of fellow diners slurping their soup. At one point, Bryan thought he would bring earplugs with him to these breakfast forays, so that he could truly enjoy his breakfast.

Finally one day, one of Bryan's joint venture partners told us the logic behind slurping. The gentleman said, "I know it is considered rude to slurp in Western cul-

ture, but I really can't drink my Chinese soup without slurping. Western soups are typically very thick and are served lukewarm. So it is possible to put a big spoonful of it into your mouth without getting burned. But Chinese soups are meant to be served piping hot. If you put a big spoonful into your mouth, you would totally get burned. But if you put just a tiny amount in at a time, you can't taste the flavor of the soup. The only way to taste the soup and not burn your mouth is to slurp. Slurping allows cool air to rush into your mouth at the same time that you take in the soup, enabling you to simultaneously drink it hot and not get burned."

Bryan and I thought his explanation was really insightful. It could explain why the only acceptable slurping (albeit very quietly) by Westerners is when they drink hot coffee. If they took too big of a gulp of a very hot beverage, they would surely burn their mouths and throats.

Although Bryan can now understand why Chinese people slurp hot soup, he still finds it difficult to get accustomed to the noisy eaters next to him.

21. Knocking on the Table

We were eating at a restaurant with some Chinese friends and one of them asked the waitress to refill his tea cup. When she finished pouring the tea, he didn't say "thank you," but instead knocked two knuckles on the table. Bryan asked him why knocking on the table meant "thank you" and our friend told us this story:

China was ruled by emperors for several thousand years. One emperor decided to travel around his empire and see for himself how the country and its citizens were doing. This was actually hard to do, however, because he had hundreds of people accompanying him everywhere and everyone prepared their best for his

arrival. Therefore, the emperor decided to travel incognito with only two trusted aides, so that he could move about freely without being recognized.

One evening during their journey, the emperor and his aides were eating dinner at a local restaurant. The aides were very nervous about eating at the same table as the emperor, because this was never, ever done. But the emperor insisted that they eat together to maintain his disguise.

When the tea arrived, the emperor did something that stunned his aides; he lifted the teapot and personally served tea to them. His aides wanted to fall to their knees and kow-tow to the emperor, which they normally would have done at the palace, but that would have blown their disguises. So instead, they each balled up their right hands into a fist, stuck out their index finger and third fingers like a pair of legs, and bent them at the first knuckle, like knees. They then tapped the "knees" on the table to signify their kow-towing! This way, they could respect their emperor without giving away his identity.

So now, if someone pours tea, beer, water, etc. for you, you can also show your thanks by tapping your knuckle "knees" on the table.

22. Fighting for the Check in Restaurants

When our friends from New York came to China for a visit, we took them to a local Chinese restaurant in our neighborhood for an authentic Chinese dining experience. The food was delicious, the staff was warm and friendly, and the crowd was just boisterous enough to make the restaurant a "happening place" without being too loud. We were having a great dining experience until we heard a loud argument erupting from the next table. Two couples of well dressed Chinese men and women were literally fighting over a little black leather notebook. They were talking excitedly, gesticulating, and grabbing the notebook from each other's hands. After listening for a few seconds, I realized that they were fighting to pay for the bill.

Our American guests were astonished until I explained this seemingly explosive situation to them. When Chinese friends get together for meals, each will try to pay for the bill as a sign of generosity. In fact, it is considered impolite not to offer to pay. People who consistently do not pay for meals are seen as misers. In Chinese, they are described by the pejorative *tie gongji* or "iron rooster" which indicates a bird which won't even pluck out one feather to pay for things.

The better the friendship, the more vigorous the fight is over the bill.

"But why don't they just go 'Dutch' and pay individually?" our friend asked. "Because," I commented, "to most Chinese, sharing the bill is very impersonal. Going 'Dutch' suggests that 'you don't owe me anything and I don't owe you anything.'" Although you might go "Dutch" when going out for lunch with colleagues, that is not what friends do in China. The social norm is to take turns and invite each other for meals. In addition, when reciprocating a dinner invitation, you would always make sure to pick restaurants of the same or higher caliber than the ones you had shared when it was their turn. This way, you make sure that your friends don't feel that you took advantage of them.

Pay For Dinner to Show That You Will Be a Good Provider

Despite living in the United States for more than two decades, my parents remain quite traditional when it comes to Chinese customs and values. This was especially true when it came to my choice of a husband. My parents automatically measured all my boyfriends according to the Chinese yardstick for sons-in-law.

Unbeknownst to me, one of the first "tests" for a future son-in-law is to see whether he volunteers to pay for dinner the first time he meets the girl's family. Accordingly, on Bryan's first visit to my parents' home in Pittsburgh, my father took us all to a nice Chinese restaurant. After the desserts were served, my father expected Bryan to offer to pay. Unfortunately for Bryan, I was not aware of the Chinese dating protocols and did not alert him ahead of time to pay the bill. When the check arrived, Bryan did not reach for the bill; instead, he respectfully said thank you to my father for inviting him to dinner. My father paid the check, but became quite solemn and distant toward Bryan for the rest of the visit.

When Bryan left, my parents told me in no uncertain terms that he was not right for me. They said that a man who would not offer to pay for dinner will not provide well for his wife in marriage. In short, they thought he was a cheapskate.

When I told Bryan my parents' comment, he was stunned. He thought he was being polite by not offering to pay. In American culture, Bryan explained, if the boyfriend of the daughter tried to pay for a meal with her parents, it would be an insult to the father. It would imply that the father couldn't afford to take his family out. He was surprised to find that the opposite is true in Chinese custom.

A few years later, after we were married, we went out to a restaurant with my parents again. Having learned his lesson the hard way, Bryan was determined to pay for all future meals with my parents. When the check came, he quickly reached out to grab it. He thought that this would show my parents how good a son-in-law he had become.

This time, however, my father told him that he was not allowed to pay. Now that Bryan had married me, my father explained to him, he had become a son to my parents. Being the most senior male at a family meal, my father would pay for the bill. If Bryan insisted upon paying, it would be a challenge to my father's position in the family.

Bryan handed over the check and sighed, "Why do the Chinese have such an opposite way of doing things from the Americans? In America, once a man is married, he becomes the head of his family and enjoys a status equal to his father-in-law's. It is therefore completely fine for him to pay for a family meal. But in Chinese culture, the son-in-law is expected to pay before but not after marriage!"

23. Restaurant Receipt Lottery

After eating at a restaurant, every new visitor to China wonders why the waiter gives them a small stack of colorful receipts when they pay their bill. Unlike Western receipts, which are typically an itemized invoice or a credit card receipt, Chinese receipts come in several colors and have silver scratchable areas on them. In fact, they resemble lottery scratch-offs. "What ARE these?" visitors often ask. That, we answer, is how the Chinese government makes sure that customers will ask for tax receipts that restaurant owners often do not want to give!

Most restaurants in China operate on a cash basis and those restaurants taking card payments prefer debit cards to credit cards. This cash economy has made it very difficult for the Chinese government to accurately tax the restaurant businesses, so it needed a system that would drive customers to ask for government-issued tax receipts from the restaurant owners.

Their answer was to put a lottery ticket on each tax receipt and to enact a regulation requiring businesses to submit these tax receipts for any meals claimed as a business expense. The lottery on these receipts makes people ask for the receipts, because although the chances of winning are small and the rewards range from five to two-hundred RMB, people still think it is lucky to win. And of course, businesses will force their employees to submit the receipts with their expense reimbursements. Both these measures made it much easier for the government to properly tax food and beverage businesses.

So the next time you eat or drink in China, try your luck by asking for and scratching the tax receipts!

24. Lukewarm Recommendations

I have a habit of asking waiters and food vendors for recommendations. For example, in a restaurant, I always ask which dish is best, and at a bakery, what cake is best. In the United States, the answer is typically straight forward and very personal, with the waiter or waitress saying "I really like this one" or "That one is my favorite."

In China, however, I find the answers are very different. If the waiter or waitress thinks that something is very good, she might say "This one is doable" (*zhe ge hai ke yi*) or "You can try this." But their recommendations are almost never enthusiastic, and are usually based on what other customers tend to order rather than their own personal opinions. For example, when I ask whether a certain meat dish is delicious, the waitress will say "A lot of customers order this" to indicate it is a good choice, and "Not many people order that" to say it is probably not worth trying.

I think there are two main reasons for such a difference in their answers.

The Chinese are usually more reserved about their personal opinions than Americans are, especially in front of strangers. Thus they will tend to be less enthusiastic in voicing personal opinions. But equally important is the fact that the American waiters tend to evaluate the food based on their own experiences because they've eaten it, whereas Chinese waiters are often not consumers of their products. Their recommendations are not based on their own experiences, but rely heavily on other customers' feedback.

IV
Everyday Etiquette
and Customs

25. Different Sizes of Personal Space

Bryan and I used to work in Times Square in New York City. The crowd there is constant; you are always surrounded by people even at two o'clock in the morning. However, despite the crush of people, we rarely ever bumped into anybody physically (unless it was New Year's Eve when you are squeezed on all sides by people waiting to watch the ball drop). People in Times Square seem to have an uncanny ability to avoid touching others. They turn their shoulders, step sideways, or even duck to navigate a narrow space without coming into physical contact with other people.

In China, the experience is quite different. We live near Xujiahui in Shanghai. It is the equivalent of Times Square in New York where shoppers and tourists congregate in huge masses. During the weekends, there is literally a sea of people in Xujiahui. Unlike in New York City, people here don't seem to mind the body contact between strangers.

One weekend, Bryan and I went to Xujiahui for some electronics shopping. As we walked on the crowded streets, people kept bumping into the two of us. And when they did, they didn't say sorry or excuse me. They just kept on walking as if nothing had happened. Bryan and I were really annoyed by this behavior. The first couple of times it happened, we turned our bodies to make more room for people to pass. By the third time, we literally stopped, turned around, and said, "Hey, watch it!" When it happened a fourth time, Bryan decided to square his shoulders and stand firm so that people who tried to pass us by bumping into Bryan's side would get bounced back. People were clearly shocked by this action. They stared at Bryan, and their face said, "I can't believe you didn't yield when we tried to pass you!" Then we began to understand why.

We finally realized that walking on crowded streets in China is just like driving bumper cars at an amusement park. The norm is to "bump with the flow." People are not trying to be rude. They simply have a different concept of personal space. For us, touching strangers in a crowd is considered invading their personal space (unless, of course, you have no choice like on a packed subway car). But in China, such personal space does not exist on busy streets.

26. Don't Leave Any Gap When You Stand in Queue!

I am used to leaving at least one foot of space between myself and others around me. So my personal space is defined by a circle with a three-foot diameter. This personal space has often proven to be too large for China. Whether

Why are you cutting in front of me?

it is in hospitals, pharmacies, or super-markets, I've repeatedly had Chinese customers cutting in queue right in front of me. When I point out to them that they should go to the end of the line, they reply, "Then why did you leave so much space in front of you? I thought you weren't part of the queue!"

27. Getting Personal

One main difference between Shanghai and New York City is that service people in Shanghai tend to stick to the letter of the law to the extent that they ignore the spirit of law.

For example, in China, restaurants and shopping malls often have greeters at the door. The purpose, I suppose, is to make customers feel welcome when they arrive and appreciated when they leave. But often these greeters fail to achieve those goals. Although they bow, say you're welcome or thank you, their facial expressions and body language exude ultimate boredom and unwillingness. Their presence actually makes customers feel uncomfortable thereby rendering the whole exercise counterproductive.

Similarly, we went to a popular hotpot restaurant in Shanghai. The wait was over thirty minutes. We were getting ravenous as it was approaching 8:30 p.m. already. So I asked the receptionist for a menu, but she insisted that they were not allowed to give customers menus until they were seated at the table. Both Bryan and I found this inflexibility surprising. After all, deciding what to order prior to sitting down benefits both the customers and the restaurant. Customers can get their food faster and the restaurant can have a faster through-put.

The way to break this rigid behavior is to get personal. Bryan was having breakfast at the JW Marriott one morning with a colleague from headquarters. When the check came, the itemized printout had a crinkle on the bottom so that the final line with the total amount paid was completely obscured. The colleague was dismayed. He said he couldn't accept a receipt like this for expense reimbursement. The waitress initially replied, "*Mei ban fa* " which meant she couldn't do anything about it.

Fortunately, Bryan had been in China long enough to know that he had to try a different tact. He had to get personal with the waitress. He told her that his colleague was the "big boss," and Bryan would be too ashamed to tell him that he couldn't get a new receipt for him. For her, if she didn't find a way to remedy the problem, then his "big boss" would have to speak to her boss, and her boss's boss. He would have to tell them that she said she couldn't do anything to fix the bad receipt. If that happened, both Bryan and the waitress would lose face.

When the situation was explained to her in such a personal way, the waitress immediately said, "Ok, let me see what I can do." Five minutes later, she came back with a brand new receipt. Not only was it perfectly legible, but it also gave the price in both RMB and Euros. The colleague was so surprised that he asked Bryan, "What did you say to her?" Bryan said, "I just put my request in more personal terms."

28. The Meaning of a Gentleman

A British friend had a first date with a Chinese woman in her late twenties. After a pleasant evening, he wished her good night, and put her into a taxi to send her home. He thought he was being a perfect gentleman to her. A few days

later, he heard from the grapevine that she was quite upset with him. She felt mistreated because he didn't get in the taxi himself to physically escort her home. He thought her resentment was ridiculous. She is an adult, perfectly capable of getting home in a taxi by herself. There was no reason for him to accompany her all the way home. A British woman would never expect that.

I had to explain to him that a Chinese boyfriend is usually a lot more protective and attentive to his girlfriend. He is expected to pick her up and drop her off at home when they go on dates. He is also expected to pay for all the taxi fares, dinner bills, and entertainment expenses. When the relationship becomes more serious, he is expected to do chores for her family. This may range from fixer-upper projects to taking care of the parents when they get sick. He literally becomes an ingratiating future son-in-law. I even know many young Chinese men who would drive all the way across the city to pick up their girlfriends, take them to work, and then drive to work themselves. At the end of the day, they would pick up the girlfriend, drop her off at her home, and then go home themselves. Given Shanghai's horrific rush-hour traffic, it could take a couple of hours to just shuttle back and forth. I joked that they have become personal slaves to the girl and her family. No wonder so many Chinese parents lament the woes of having sons!

Lucky to be the Foreign Son-in-Law

When we first bought a house in New York, my father volunteered to help us on some home improvement projects. But he fully expected Bryan to behave like the perfect Chinese son-in-law: to hold his tool kit for him, to anticipate my father's needs, and to praise him for the beautiful workmanship. Well, let's just say that Bryan didn't meet his expectations. My father had to sigh and resign himself to the fact that he has an American son-in-law. And I told Bryan how lucky he was not to be Chinese. He would have had a terrible time living up to those expectations of a proper Chinese son-in-law!

29. Girls Holding Hands?

When I took a European friend on a tour in Shanghai, he asked me surreptitiously, "Are there a lot of lesbians in China?" "Why would you ask that?" I queried. "Well," he explained, "I see a lot of girls holding hands and linking arms when they walk on the street." "Oh! No, not at all!" I laughed.

I had, in fact, become so used to seeing women walking hand in hand in China that I didn't even notice it anymore!

In China, holding hands and walking arm-in-arm with people of the same sex is not indicative of homosexuality. Instead, it is a sign of closeness among friends. You will often find girls holding hands as they walk and shop together. The gesture tells everyone that they are best friends. You will also see mothers and grown-up daughters linking arms on a shopping trip. In fact, it would be unusual to find Chinese mothers and daughters walking independently from each other. They will have at least one part of their body touching each other, whether it is one hand resting on another's arm, or the shoulders rubbing each other.

Similarly, it is also socially acceptable for men to wrap arms around each others' shoulders while walking down the street. It simply says they are best male buddies. Body contact among males, in fact, does not diminish a person's manliness. On the contrary, most often it is the most manly and athletic Chinese males who wrap arms around each other's shoulders.

30. Gentlemen First

Bryan and I went to an upscale Western restaurant with an American couple who came to China for a short visit. When we sat down, the Chinese waiter poured water for our male guest first, served Bryan second, and then poured for the ladies last. As he started pouring, our friend indicated that he should serve the ladies first, but to no avail. When the appetizers arrived, the waiter again tried to serve the gentlemen before the ladies. Our male guest became quite angry with the waiter. He said to him sharply, "Please serve the ladies first."

When the waiter left the table, Bryan and I explained to our friend why the waiter kept trying to serve him first. By Chinese custom, the waiters will first serve the most senior male by social ranking and age. In our case, our friend was the most senior male at the table, so he was served first. The most junior female is typically served last. In this case, I was the last to receive my food. The Western concept of "ladies first" does not apply in China.

Similarly, when you enter through a door or into an elevator, the most junior staff is expected to open and hold doors while the senior members enter in the order of their social ranking, regardless of whether they are male or female. When two people are of the same rank, then the older person gets the seniority.

One female Chinese government official commented that she only realizes she is a woman when she travels in Western countries, because there she is treated like a lady. In China, she is treated as one of the men in a predominantly male profession. No one would open doors for her just because she is a woman; instead, people would give her proper respects according to her rank and seniority.

31. Arriving Late, Leaving Early

Shortly after we arrived in Shanghai, one of Bryan's staff invited us to his wedding. Being the boss, Bryan was the guest of honor at this wedding banquet, which he correctly guessed meant that he had to give a brief speech and show his respects to the wedding couple and their families. But it turned out that there was another etiquette which was also very important: arriving later and leaving earlier than most other guests.

As the guest of honor, Bryan (and I) was not expected to arrive early at the big banquet. For example, if the Chinese wedding banquet starts at six o'clock in the evening, most people will show up around five-thirty, but we should not. We were expected to arrive just before the formal ceremony which began at six.

We also should not stay until the party is over, because leaving early is a sign of importance. The highest ranking individual and their family members must leave a banquet first. Only after he or she has left, can the other guests start to bid their farewells.

Given that it was our first Chinese wedding experience, Bryan and I wanted to stay and see the whole thing. But we noticed that people were uncomfortable to really party hard with the boss being there. So we left much earlier than we wanted to. The next day we were told that the real party started after our departure. I guess that's one of the hidden downsides of being the boss in China— what a bummer!

32. Ring, Ring, Go Ahead, Answer the Phone

Bryan's big boss from Germany is the CEO of a multi-billion dollar company. He comes to China a few times a year for important board meetings with their various joint venture partners.

During one formal meeting in Shanghai with the most senior Chinese partner, the discussion was heated but respectful, and the big boss was making his key points about the joint venture's next steps. In the middle of his speech, however, the Chinese partner's mobile phone rang. The Germans and Americans in the room expected he would immediately turn off the phone and apologize for the interruption. At the same time, they all made a quick check of their own mobile phones to make sure they were switched off.

Much to the Westerners' surprise, the Chinese partner didn't turn off the phone and actually had a two-minute conversation with the caller. The German CEO was dismayed. He thought the Chinese partner was being rude and disrespectful to him by answering his mobile phone in the middle of an important meeting. Although all the agenda items were discussed in the meeting, it did not end on a warm and friendly note.

After the board meeting, Bryan explained to his boss that it is not considered rude in China to answer the phone during meetings. The Chinese partner was not trying to be disrespectful by talking on the mobile phone. He simply did it out of habit. And he probably did not know it would be seen as rude.

The following year, when the same German CEO came to China, he had learned not to be upset by Chinese partners talking on mobile phones during meetings. In fact, when he attended a banquet given by the Chinese partners,

he did not switch off his own phone. When the phone rang, he said "Excuse me," and went on to answer the call just like the Chinese would. He had quickly adapted to the Chinese practice!

Cellular Phones and Nora Jones

Bryan and I went to Nora Jones' concert in China a couple years ago. The indoor arena where she performed was packed with fans, most of them Chinese.

Despite the pre-concert announcement to turn off mobile phones, many people still had them switched on. A few times the jazzy tunes were interrupted by ringing mobile phones. At first, the good-natured artist just ignored the disturbance and carried on. But when one loud ring went off in the middle of a soft and soothing piano solo, Nora Jones finally got annoyed and stopped playing. She waited for the ringing to stop. Less than a minute after she resumed playing, another phone went off. This time, she stopped, shook her head and smiled at the ridiculous situation.

While some other divas would have angrily stomped off the stage, the soft spoken singer looked toward the direction of the ring and asked, "Aren't you going to answer that?" Meanwhile, many fans, Chinese and foreigners alike booed the person whose phone was ringing. Perhaps because of her gracefulness and humor, the rest of the concert went on without further mobile phone interruptions.

33. Keep the Pants On!

Europeans and Americans are quite used to undressing completely for oil massages in the West. In China, however, this habit can cause quite an embarrassment.

I was at my favorite professional massage parlor one night and noticed that the receptionist was quite flustered. Since I am a frequent customer at that establishment, she confided in me what had happened. A European male customer had stripped stark naked in the treatment room. The massage therapist, who was a girl in her early twenties, fled the room with her face crimson red. The receptionist, who is unmarried and quite young herself but was the only person who could speak English, had to go in and tell him to at least put some under pants on. Much to her surprise and dismay, he challenged her as to why he couldn't be naked, since that was the norm in his home country. The receptionist had to tell him that nudity is not allowed according to Chinese law. This is why the massage parlors give customers loose fitting pajamas to wear. This way, the pants can be rolled all the way up for leg massage. And for upper body massages, customers can easily slip off the pajama tops to allow the masseuse to massage their back, and slip the top back on when they flip their bodies.

The massage parlor staff also finds it a bit bizarre that European girls walk around the co-ed, public areas of the massage parlor wearing only panties and brassiers. I asked if the staff asks them to get properly dressed as well. The receptionist told me, "No. At least they are not naked. If they don't mind exposing themselves, they can go ahead."

Explanatory Note:

In addition to the 'no nudity' rule, the Chinese government has also decreed that no professional massage parlors are allowed to have individual private rooms that are completely secluded from the public area. That is, there must be an opening or a window from which the inside of the private room can be seen by people outside. They can, however, have private rooms for two or three people. These rules are there to make sure that the massage places are legitimate and are not used as a front for prostitution.

This rule does not seem to apply to Western style spas in China. I have been to quite a few spas in upscale hotels or private clubs that have individual treatment rooms for massages. I suppose the rules must be different for spas. On the other hand, the prices you pay for massages at these spas are much higher than the Chinese style professional massage parlors. They are as expensive as those in the West. Furthermore, at these spas, you can be completely nude during the massage services. The masseuse covers your private areas with a towel just like they do in the West. I guess you pay for the privacy and the privilege to be nude in these more expensive spas.

34. Sneezing vs."Honking"

The Chinese often find it puzzling that when Westerners sneeze, they immediately say "Excuse me" afterwards. And their friends would reply, "God bless you" in response. The Chinese don't understand why one should apologize for sneezing; after all, it is not something one does on purpose.

On the other hand, they find it quite offensive that Westerners don't have any qualms about blowing their nose loudly in public. A few of my Chinese friends tell me that they think it is rather gross how Westerners, both male and female, blow their noses loudly into a handkerchief and then stuff the dirty

rag back in their pocket. The Chinese, on the other hand, tend to blow their noses as quietly as possible into a tissue and then quickly dispose of the dirty tissue.

I used to make fun of my mom who blows her nose so delicately that it almost looks like she is just sniffing the tissue. And she would admonish me for blowing mine hard and would warn me not to blow my brains out! I would often put a dirty tissue in a pocket until I could find a trash can at a convenient time; but she would hold a soiled tissue out between two fingers and hunt down a trash can to dispose of it.

35. Right of Way

Many foreigners feel that driving a car in China is quite difficult and do not want to drive themselves. However, my husband loves to drive (he says that Americans are born with a steering wheel in their hands), and has been driving in Shanghai for the past two years.

Bryan comments on driving in Shanghai: "A lot of my friends think the driving here is too dangerous because of all the bicyclists and pedestrians, but actually, I feel that driving here in China is no more dangerous than driving in, say, New York. I drove for more than five years in New York City which gave me great training. Still, as long as you understand that the rules of the road are slightly different in China, you will be fine."

In particular, one of the most fundamental rules in driving—who has the right of way—is different in China than in the West. Understanding this makes it a lot safer for Westerners to drive here. In the West, the car that is going straight has the right of way over cars that are turning left. So, if you're driving straight through an intersection, a car in the opposing lane wanting to turn left—therefore in front of you—would wait for you to go through. This is not the case in China.

Very often cars will turn left in front of cars that are going straight, expecting the latter cars to stop. Additionally, cars that are entering the highway or a road from the right in the West will typically wait until any car going straight on the road has gone by. Once again, the car going straight has the right of way and cars coming in from the right must yield. But, in China, it is very typical for cars to enter the roadway without looking to see if they have room to merge. The assumption is that the car going straight, which in the West would have the right of way, will see them and will avoid them. You also have to watch for bicyclists and motorcyclists who drive onto roads suddenly and expect the traffic to slow down for them. The rationale may very well be that, if a vehicle coming in from the right were to wait until the way was clear, he would never get onto the road.

Once I understood that the fundamental principle of right of way was different (or ignored), my driving became a lot more defensive, but also a lot safer. I learned to know what the other drivers intended to do. This may not be the law in China, but it is what happens in practice. You just have to be prepared for this reality.

36. Hang Your Laundry Out

One day I asked an American lady who recently moved to China how she liked living here. She said, "My apartment is great on the inside, but I hate it from the outside. I am so embarrassed to tell my friends that I live in a building where people hang their laundry out on the balcony to dry."

Meanwhile at home, both my mother and our Chinese housekeeper keep complaining to me that our apartment does not have a big enough balcony to hang our clothes out to dry. Instead, we have to rely mostly on our dryer or hang the semi-wet clothes on a rack inside the apartment.

One day I mentioned to our housekeeper that, in the United States, we never dry our clothes outside on a clothes line. Everything is dried in the dryer. I tell them that it is considered uncivilized to hang one's undergarments out in public. She was shocked. "What? You never dry your underwear in the sun? How can it be clean then? You need the sun and its ultra-violet rays to kill the bacteria on the underwear." I was not able to convince her that the washers and dryers do an adequate job cleaning our clothes.

Now we compromise. We first leave the clothes in the dryer to get semi-dry so that they don't drip, then our housekeeper finds a sunny patch in the apartment to dry them on the cloth rack.

37. Parks at Night Are for Lovers

When Bryan and I lived in Manhattan, we would go for a nice walk in the park on pleasant nights. We would bring our dog along while pushing the baby stroller as we walked. At the park, we would see other families walking their babies and dogs, or late night runners and roller-bladers getting in their exercise before the day ended.

When we first moved to China, we tried to do that at first but quickly learned not to do it here.

It was a cool autumn night and Bryan and I decided to take a detour through the park after a big dinner to walk off some

of the calories. The parks in China are dimly lit so we didn't notice anything when we first walked in. Slowly as our eyes adjusted to the dark surroundings, we saw many couples in intimate positions on the park benches. Often there were three couples to each park bench. As we walked, we saw that not only the benches, but every available sitting space was occupied by couples in love. We were so embarrassed to have intruded into this intimate space that we literally did not know where to look. So we lowered our heads and focused only on the two feet in front of us and walked briskly out of the park. The area near the park entrance was brightly lit with fluorescent stadium lights. There we found the older people and young children playing. They had vacated the park for the lovers.

In China, parks belong to the old, the kids, and the families by day, but belong to the lovers by night!

38. The Old Ladies Cheered Me On!

Shanghai hosts a marathon competition every November. Two years ago, Bryan and his buddies decided to run the half marathon here. Despite his good intentions, he didn't have a chance to train for the race before the day arrived. So I asked him to run the 5K fun race instead. But boys will be boys. Fearful of his male running friends making fun of him and driven by his testosterone, Bryan decided to run the half marathon without any preparation.

The first ten kilometers went very well, so he thought it was no big deal to just run another ten or so. But slowly, each additional kilometer became more and more difficult. He thought about quitting and began to walk in between spurts of runs. The only thing that kept him running was the old ladies at each kilometer mark.

In the New York City marathon, there will be tons of people cheering and volunteering at various mile markers. Often these are friends and families of the runners. In China, the cheerleaders are the retired ladies and sometimes old men from various nearby neighborhoods. They wear bright red outfits and dance with drums and gongs. Every time they see a runner nearing the kilometer mark,

they start a dance routine and shout *"jia you, jia you!"* which literally means "add gas, add gas!" to cheer the runners on. Even when Bryan became utterly exhausted, he would always pick up his pace as he passed in front of the old ladies. Their enthusiasm really kept him going.

In China, you can find these retired men and women practicing their songs and dances on many street corners and in many parks in the early morning, in the evening, and on weekends. Their activities range from ballroom dancing to martial arts, from *taiqi* to choir practice. They always seem to be focused and having fun doing these activities. For them, these activities are not only a fun way to socialize with friends and neighbors, but are excellent forms of exercise which keep them healthy and fit in their old age.

39. Singing with Your Friends

Karaoke, or singing with a group of friends or colleagues, is extremely popular in China. Many of our Western friends are surprised when they hear this, and are even more surprised when they hear that Bryan and I enjoy it. Karaoke is not especially popular in most Western countries, so our friends ask us why it is so popular here.

Our explanation is that the Chinese tend to be modest, quiet and discreet in their work and social lives, and singing gives them a chance to loosen up and show off what they've got in front of their friends. Karaoke rooms can seat ten or more people, so it is a great venue for large groups, and everyone can have a drink, play dice or other games, and sing their favorite songs. Bryan likes to go to karaoke with business colleagues or venture partners to show that their relationship is more than just work, and also to let them see that he's got a few songs (but only a few) that he can really belt out.

Many of our Western friends reply that they would never want to sing in front of others because they would be too embarrassed. Interestingly, however, they would have no problem giving a presentation in front of an audience, or speaking up at a company meeting. Many Chinese, on the other hand, would be hesitant to speak in public, but wouldn't hesitate to sing karaoke in front of their friends. People express themselves in very different ways!

40. Bathrobes on the Beach

Our favorite vacation spot in China is Sanya, the southernmost tropical city on Hainan Island. The first time we went down there, we saw all the Chinese vacationers wearing their bathrobes on the beach, by the pool, and in other public areas. At first we found this behavior very strange, as you almost never see anyone wearing bathrobes outside of their rooms in Western resorts. Then as we walked around the resort, we saw pictures of several senior Chinese officials visiting the resort grounds in their hotel bathrobes. We concluded that that was why all the Chinese tourists wore their bathrobes in the resort. If their leaders did so, it must be okay for them to do the same.

In fact, we had two sets of bathrobes in our hotel room. One set was made of terrycloth and was for wearing in the room after showering. Another set was made of thin cotton, and those are the ones we saw people wearing outside of their rooms (the same one that the officials had worn in the pictures).

During our most recent trip to Sanya, we even saw Western tourists wearing their bathrobes by the pool. I guess they must have picked up the local fashion as well!

41. She Can't Hear What She Does Not Understand

At home, I speak English with my husband, Mandarin to my children, and Shanghai dialect to our nanny. Most of the time, I am able to switch languages from sentence to sentence. But it gets really tricky when two of them start speaking at the same time.

One interesting phenomenon I observed is that each person tends to filter out the languages he or she doesn't understand.

Bryan and I were having a nice dinner conversation one night at home. As Bryan was speaking with me, however, our nanny abruptly launched into a conversation with me about our son. Bryan stopped mid-sentence, and stared at her, utterly astounded by how rude she was at interrupting him. Meanwhile, our nanny was completely oblivious to Bryan's anger. She continued her story without even the slightest pause. For her, our English conversation was like background noise and she seemed to have no idea that she had interrupted us. So, after responding to her briefly, I had to explain to Bryan that she didn't mean to interrupt at all. She just simply couldn't "hear" what she didn't understand.

Similarly, Bryan inadvertently interrupts my conversation with the nanny sometimes because he didn't realize we were talking. His brain had automatically filtered out Shanghai dialect as irrelevant background noise. So when that happens, I pause my conversation with our nanny, ask Bryan to please "hold that thought," and then finish my talk with the nanny.

A couple of times, I have tried to carry on two conversations at once because I thought one of them would be brief. But that tactic failed both times. Both of them got really annoyed at me for not giving them 100% of my attention. Now, when both of them start talking at the same time, I interrupt them both and point out, with a laugh, their "deafness" to each other's foreign language.

V
Beliefs

42. Big Ears and Fleshy Noses Are Lucky

Whenever Chinese people meet our children, they pay special attention to their ears. They either compliment our son on his big ears and large ear lobes or praise our daughter for having perfectly formed ears for a girl.

It turns out that big ears with thick and large ear lobes are auspicious signs. People who have them are thought to be very lucky in life. They are likely to have happy childhoods and become successful adults. Similarly, if someone has a fleshy nose, he is likely to be well off financially in his forties and fifties. When I asked people why they believe that, they say, "Look at the Happy Buddha, he has huge ear lobes and a fleshy nose!"

This is why many Chinese people will look at someone's nose and ears to see whether that person is lucky. Even some of Bryan's Chinese joint venture partners would comment on Bryan's facial features. One partner told Bryan during their first face-to-face meeting that he trusts Bryan and can foresee a good working relationship ahead because Bryan has a rounded face, a fleshy nose, and big ear lobes.

The funny thing is, now we begin to notice people's ear lobes and noses.

Much to my surprise, when I browsed through Forbes magazine's richest individuals in the world, I saw almost all of them have big ear lobes. Bryan joked that he should pull on his ear lobes everyday to make himself even luckier!

43. Colors and Traditions

Red

Red is the color of auspiciousness or good fortune. This is why the traditional Chinese wedding colors are red. The bride is dressed in a red *qipao*, or long form-fitting gown. The groom wears a big red sash with a bow over his long black gown. (Nowadays, many brides and grooms also wear white wedding gowns and tuxedos like in the West, but they will always have a traditional Chinese red costume to change into after the formal exchange of vows.)

Babies and anything associated with fertility is also symbolized by red. For example, a new mother will give out hard-boiled eggs dyed red to all her friends. In this way she is thought to pass on her fertility and good fortune to them.

Additionally, red is thought to ward off evil and bad luck. The Chinese believe that one is typically unlucky in the zodiac year in which one was born. For example, if you are born in the year of the dog, then every dog year is considered especially dangerous for you. In order to protect themselves in their zodiac year, many Chinese wear bright red underwear all year round. So the next time you see red underwear flying on a clothes line, you can bet the resident was born in the current zodiac year.

White

White is a color most often associated with funerals. Funeral homes are decorated with white flowers and wreaths. White flowers are given to the family of the deceased as a sign of condolence. Thus it is crucial not to give white flowers to Chinese friends, especially not as a gift to someone who is sick.

My Western friend's cleaning lady suffered a sudden illness, so my friend brought a beautiful bunch of white lilies to the hospital for her. The cleaning lady was very uncomfortable with the gift, but she did not explain to my friend why. Only days later, after she was released from the hospital, did the cleaning lady tell my friend the problem. She was fearful because one only gives white flowers when someone dies or is likely to die.

In addition to giving white flowers, it is also taboo to wear white in one's hair. When I was a little girl, I bought myself a piece of hair elastic with two white pearl balls on it. It was summer and I thought it would go nicely with my outfit. That summer while I was visiting my paternal grandmother in Shanghai, my father noticed my hair accessory. He was horrified. In a stern voice, he ordered me to take it off immediately. Then he explained to me that white is a funerary color, and wearing it in my hair meant that one of my parents or grandparents has just passed away. Furthermore, wearing white in the hair when no one has died is considered very unlucky. In fact, it is even thought to precipitate an untimely death of a family member. So, needless to say, I took that hair elastic off and stored it way deep in my cosmetic drawer.

Black

Black is a somber color in Chinese. It signifies formality and is also a funerary color. When attending a funeral, friends and distant relatives all wear black (whereas white is reserved for the immediate family). And for months after the funeral, children of the deceased often wear a black cloth armband to indicate mourning. The grandchildren, however, have a small red square stapled on their black armband. The little red square indicates that the deceased had lived long enough to have grandchildren, so it is a symbol of fortune and longevity.

Green

Green is typically an innocuous color. The only thing to be aware of is not to give anyone, especially a man, a green hat as a gift. A green hat on a man indicates he is a cuckold. Calling someone a turtle also means the same.

44. Numbers and Meanings

In many Western countries, there is often no 13th floor in hotels and residential buildings. Thirteen has been considered an unlucky number for centuries. Additionally, the number 666 has a connection to the devil. Well, the Chinese are superstitious about a few numbers as well.

Four

The number "4" is an unlucky number in Chinese. The word "four" is a homonym for the noun "death" or the verb "to die." Therefore, some Chinese prefer not to live at places that have a number "4" in the address. One of my good local Shanghaiese friends, while house hunting, didn't even want to go inside to look at the beautiful garden of a house that had a number "4" in the street address. She explained to me that her husband would rather live in a house numbered "13" than one numbered "4". By the same token, numbers like "14" and "44" are also inauspicious and avoided. Some hotels in China now don't even have a 44th floor because many Chinese guests would not want to stay on it.

Eight

The number "8", on the other hand, is a very lucky number. It sounds like the word "getting rich" in Chinese, especially in Cantonese. Therefore, businesses love to have the number "8" in any part of their address or phone number. They believe that the usage of the number "8" will actually bring them good luck and prosperity. In fact, people will spend more money to buy phone numbers and license plates that contain "8". So if you see a license plate that has the number "8" for all its numerals, you can be sure the person is a businessman who spent a fortune for it! Similarly, a real estate property with an "8" in its address will be in greater demand.

Six

The number 6 is also a favorable number. It sounds like the word "happiness" in Chinese. When Bryan and I lived in Manhattan, our building address began with "666". Most of our Western friends made fun of us for living at the devil's address. But all of our Chinese friends (and I) thought the address was great. It stood for triple happiness.

Thirty-eight

Beware of the number "38". It is especially problematic when associated with women. In Chinese parlance, "38" or *"sanba"* is a pejorative for women. It can mean bitchy, bimbo-like, trampy, or shameless depending upon the context. So it is definitely not good for any woman to be called *"sanba"*. Ironically, March 8th, 3/8, is the International Day of Women. It is a day when all Chinese women can take a half day off from work. Stores and restaurants have special bargains for women on that day. I don't know if there is any relationship between March 8th and the pejorative word. Just be sure you make a clear distinction between March 8th the noun and "38" the adjective when you do say the word *"sanba "* in Chinese.

The Play of Numbers

The interesting thing about numbers in Chinese is that you can easily transform a number into a completely different word by slightly changing its pronunciation. It certainly makes memorizing numbers easier. For example, "1" sounds like the verb "want", "9" is identical to the word "wine" or "liquor". Similarly, the number "5" can sound like the word "I" or "me". And the number "7" sounds like the verb "eat." When combined, the number "57" sounds like the phrase "I eat." There is a clever commercial played in many Shanghai taxis that advertise for a service which makes restaurant recommendations and reservations. The phone number for that service is 57-57-5777. "I eat, I eat, I eat eat eat!"

45. Animals and Symbols

Fish

Fish are one of the most ubiquitous items in Chinese paintings, gardens, and interior decor. Most Chinese hotels, restaurants, and families keep a fish pond or tanks that contain beautiful gold fish or brightly colored koi. And during holiday celebrations, you can always find fish as a main entrée.

The popularity of fish comes from the fact that the word for fish, *yu*, is a homonym for "extra." Therefore, people believe having fish in their home or their workplace will help them get a little extra income or profit.

Over the past decade, as the Chinese economy has soared and the number of restaurants mushroomed in cities, more and more business entrepreneurs try to increase their luck in the increasingly competitive environment. Therefore, having the right kind of fish in their display cases becomes important. In recent years, one particular kind of goldfish became very popular among restaurant owners (for show, not for eating!). It is a special breed called "get rich fish."

These goldfish are bright orange. They have such a rotund body that they look like balloons ready to pop. Their owners typically pack hundreds of them into one giant rectangular tank. Both their individual butterball look and their sheer number represent abundance in the literal sense. Their obese bodies show that they are clearly well-fed, and their large number means the restaurant is going to have lots of "extras." As if that is not enough, I have seen some ingenious aquarium shops tattoo the characters *fa tsai*, "get rich," onto individual fish bodies. These tattoos even glow in the dark!

Dragons and Phoenix

Dragons and phoenix are mystical creatures that are both powerful and auspicious. In dynastic days, the dragon symbolized the emperor. But today, one sees dragons and phoenix most often at weddings. The dragon represents the groom and phoenix the bride. In more traditional families, the newlyweds receive silk beddings (from the parents) that have dragons and phoenix embroidered on them. Wedding halls are often named after the two creatures and are decorated with their themes. Sometimes even the chinaware for the newlyweds has dragons and phoenix painted on them.

In Chinese parlance, dragon and phoenix also represent the pinnacle of achievement for men and women. Parents' hope for their sons is expressed in the phrase *wang zi cheng long*, which means "wishing the son to become a dragon." Similarly, their hope for daughters is encapsulated in the phrase *wang nü cheng feng*, "wishing the daughter to become a phoenix."

Finally, as you may already know, the dragon is the symbol of China. The Chinese consider themselves descendents of the dragon. This is an identity shared by Chinese people living in China, as well as people of Chinese descent throughout the world.

Mandarin Ducks

Another symbol associated with Chinese weddings and anniversaries is the mandarin duck. Their unique green-blue heads and brown and black colored feathers are seen in wedding decorations and on dishes, etc. The lifelong partnership of the mandarin ducks symbolizes the couple's loyalty and love for each other. For that reason, paintings or artwork of mandarin ducks are perfect gifts for weddings or important anniversaries. They are both celebrations and reminders of the couple's life long commitment to each other.

Cranes

Cranes are symbols of longevity most often seen in Chinese brush paintings or as bronze statues in traditional gardens. They are often paired with pine trees, also a symbol of strength and longevity. In addition, cranes were symbols of non-military officials in the late dynastic China. Cranes were embroidered on official robes to indicate an individual's status.

Turtles

Turtles live to be hundreds of years old; therefore, they are another symbol of longevity for the Chinese. Turtles symbolize longevity, so they are a suitable gift for young and old alike. However, one has to be careful not to call anyone, especially a man, a turtle. Calling a man a "turtle" means his wife is cheating on him. And that is definitely not a good thing to say!

Bats

Bats appear frequently in Chinese jewelry design, especially in jade pendants and gold charms. That is because the word for bats, *bian fu*, sounds like the word luck, *fu*, in Chinese. Therefore, in Chinese culture, there are none of the dark associations with bats typical of Western cultures. In fact, it is very auspicious to wear a pendant with bat carvings on it because it will bring you good luck!

Tigers

You may encounter paintings or embroideries of tigers as you wander through art galleries and shopping stalls in China. The tiger is a powerful animal and is typically associated with military or physical might in traditional Chinese culture. In the Qing dynasty, only high ranking military officers wore tigers on their robes (when they were not in combat uniform). This was an indication of their rank and position. And families would not usually put a painting of tiger in their living room. A large painting of a tiger in the main hall of a household indicates that the man of the house is a military official.

46. Fruity Symbolism

Apples

Apples symbolize safety and peace in China because the Chinese word for apple, *ping guo*, shares the same sound as the word for safety, *ping an*. Accordingly, apples are a welcome fruit in winter, especially during Chinese New Year celebrations. Most families will have a big plate of apples on prominent display. By having apples at home, the Chinese hope to have a New Year free of troubles and turbulence.

My grandmother used to build a large pyramid of apples during Chinese New Year. She placed this in front of the picture of my grandfather (who passed away many years ago). She did this to wish him safety and happiness in his world and to ask him to watch out for us and keep us safe and sound. During the New Year celebrations, we would bow in front of my grandfather's picture to pay him our love and respect.

Pears

Pears are not used as gifts or displays during Chinese holidays. This is because pears are called *li* in Chinese and this is the same sound as the word for "separation." Therefore, it is traditionally bad luck to have pears during family celebrations and holidays.

Interestingly, pears can have a very different meaning outside of China. One of my best friends in the United States gave out beautifully wrapped pears as wedding favors. At first I was perplexed, but then I realized her wittiness in this gesture—"pear" sounds just like "pair" which is perfectly appropriate for a wedding where a pair comes together. How funny that the same fruit can have such an opposite meaning in two different cultures!

Peaches

Peaches are another great fruit to display during Chinese festivities. The Chinese believe peaches are one of the healthiest fruits a person can eat, and that they will extend one's lifespan if eaten regularly. For that reason, peaches are a symbol of longevity. They are great gifts for elderly people because they serve to wish them a long and healthy life.

(Incidentally, plums and apricots are believed to be very harmful. One folklore story says that "peaches nourish, plums harm, and apricots bury!")

Pomegranates

Well, it is easy to figure out why pomegranates are lucky fruits! Its many seeds mean fertility in China. Traditionally, the Chinese believe it is a blessing to have many children and grandchildren. Even today, despite the government's "one-child" policy for each couple, it is still a good gesture to give pomegranates as gifts to newlywed couples.

47. Birthday Celebrations

Bryan and a Western colleague wanted to celebrate their Chinese HR director's birthday. Due to hectic schedules, they missed her actual birthday. A couple weeks later, Bryan asked his assistant to arrange a belated birthday dinner. His assistant immediately replied, "But her birthday has already passed!" Bryan said, " That's OK. We will still have the birthday dinner for her."

On the night of the dinner, the Western colleague toasted a "Happy birthday" to the birthday girl. Instead of accepting the toast, she immediately added, "Let's toast to my 7th anniversary at the company!" She later explained that the Chinese do not celebrate birthdays after the actual date is over. Birthdays can only be celebrated on or before the actual date. That was why she had to toast to her seven years of service to the company instead.

Bryan was surprised by that custom, because in America, birthdays can only be celebrated on or after the actual date. If you have a birthday party before the actual date, people might think that you want to wheedle an extra party and gifts out of the occasion. Some people also believe that it is bad luck to wish someone happy birthday before they reach that day.

48. Unusual Birthdays

While most birthdays are celebrated with noodles and cakes in China, there are a few unusual birthdays that Chinese people treat differently.

There are a couple birthdays that people do not celebrate. In fact, it is considered bad luck to celebrate them. For women, the 30th birthday is not celebrated. Like in the West, turning thirty is a big milestone in a woman's life.

For many Chinese, it is a period of uncertainty and danger when mishaps often take place. In order to avoid bad luck, Chinese women often do not celebrate their 30th birthday, remaining twenty-nine for two years and skipping right to thirty-one. This way, they hope the 30th year will go by quietly and without any troubles. For men, the unlucky year is forty. Many Chinese men do not celebrate their 40th birthday just like the women do not celebrate their 30th.

In addition to the 30th and 40th birthdays, 33rd and 66th birthdays are also occasions to be careful of and cautious. These two years are thought to be potentially dangerous and troublesome, especially for women. In order to warn off evil, women turning thirty-three must buy a piece of meat on her birthday, hide behind the kitchen door while chopping the meat thirty-three times, and throw it away. It is believed that doing so will cast all the evil spirits into the meat so that the year can pass by smoothly. One of our good Chinese friends had a terrible year a couple of years ago when she was thirty-three. She had fallen sick quite a few times and had a lot of headaches at work. She finally remembered that she had forgotten to cut the meat thirty-three times on her birthday. Having had enough of bad things happening to her, she decided to do the ritual even though her birthday had passed. I don't know if her year improved markedly, but she was relieved to have at least located the cause of her bad luck and be able to do something about it.

Similarly, the 66th year in a woman's life is also precarious. On a woman's 66th birthday, her daughter, if she has one, must buy a piece of meat and cut it sixty-six times in the kitchen to get rid of bad luck. If she does not have a daughter, then her daughter-in-law or another younger female relative can do the deed. For example, when my grandmother turned sixty-six, I cut the meat for her because I was the closest female relative present at the time. Even though there was no way to prove the effectiveness of my actions, my grandmother really appreciated my gesture and my good intentions. And I was glad she had a really happy birthday!

VI
Food and Drink

49. No Cold Water for Guests

We have a good German friend who speaks very good Chinese. She travels around China frequently for business and meets with many local Chinese business partners. The first year she came to China, she kept asking for cold water at business meetings. But inevitably, she would get either boiling water or green tea back as a drink.

There is a two-fold reason for that:

First, most Chinese would not serve plain water to their guests because it is seen as too simple and too bland (only family members are offered plain water).

Second, cold drinking water is not always available. Before the days of bottled water, most people in China obtain cold water by boiling tap water (not portable in China) first, and then let it cool to room temperature. Although in recent years, more and more people began to drink bottled mineral water, in smaller towns and provincial places, bottled water is still considered a luxury item. When guests come, they are accustomed to serve hot tea using boiled tap water. When the guests don't drink tea, they can only offer them hot boiled water as an alternative.

Over the years, our friend tells us that she no longer asks for cold water at Chinese business meetings. In fact, she now finds herself pouring hot water into her mug even when she works alone in her office. That, she says, is a sign that she's finally settled here.

50. How Do I Drink Green Tea?

Normally in Europe, when you drink tea, it comes in tea cups with either pre-packaged tea bags or with loose tea in a strainer. But in China, green tea is served in tall clear glasses with just loose leaves floating on the top.

One western colleague didn't know how she was supposed to drink it. No matter how much you try to blow the leaves away from your mouth, they keep rushing back to your lips as soon as you start sipping the water. If you clamp your lips tightly around the rim of the glass, the wet tea leaves tend to stick to your lips and make you look very silly. Eventually, to avoid embarrassment, our friend drank the tea and just swallowed the tea leaves.

As she stayed in China longer, she observed how the Chinese drink green tea. There are basically three ways. First, some Chinese drink the tea with the leaves. They chew and then swallow the leaves. Second, some slurp the tea, using their front teeth as a filtering device to block out the tea leaves. Finally, others drink the tea and spit out the tea leaves in a small plate. All three methods are completely acceptable culturally.

Although initially our friend found it a bit uncomfortable to spit out the tea leaves—as it is not polite in western culture to spit out anything once it is inside one's mouth—eventually she adopted the local custom. Now she can drink green tea like a Chinese and can conduct business meetings with local Chinese partners without giving a thought to the loose tea leaves floating in the glass.

51. Beer, Red Wine, or Hard Liquor?

Like most cultures, the Chinese drink different kinds of alcohol at different occasions.

Beer is a casual drink among friends, families, and colleagues. The Chinese can drink beer in copious amounts. I remember when I came to China as a college student one summer. My friends at the Chinese universities would order a huge bottle of beer for each person. I was surprised to find that a big bottle of local beer was a lot less expensive than a bottle of water at that time.

Red wine is the drink of choice when you meet with senior officials in the government or with important clients for the first time. It is seen as a more elegant drink. One would usually order an expensive bottle of red wine but would sip it slowly. It is not a drink one would go "bottoms up" in toasts. It is not unusual, however, to see Chinese add ice cubes and Sprite to their glasses of red wine. Bryan and I had a business lunch with the head of a big publishing house in Beijing a couple of years ago. We ordered a nice bottle of Chinese-made red wine for our guest. The gentleman asked for ice cubes and some Sprite to put into the wine. It was the first time we had seen that done, so out of respect, both of us quickly added ice cubes and Sprite to our glasses as well.

The hard liquor known as "*bai jiu*" is favored by people in northern China. It is a very strong grain alcohol which can be upwards of 120-proof. People typically drink this hard alcohol for two reasons. First, it is a way to loosen up. Getting a little drunk is not a social embarrassment in China. On the contrary, allowing yourself to get a little drunk is a sign that you are lowering your inhibitions and are becoming friends with your drinking partners. In northern China, friendships are cemented after you have gotten drunk with your Chinese business partners. Second, offering hard liquor is a business strategy to get the other to agree to otherwise difficult business terms. If one is drunk, he is more likely to say "yes" to things he would not have when sober.

After attending a few dinners with Chinese business partners, Bryan commented that fortunately he had a high level of alcohol tolerance from when he

was the president of a fraternity house in college. On most occasions, he can out-drink his Chinese colleagues, or at least hold his own, and this has helped him establish both friendships and credibility with his associates.

52. It's Better If You Cook It

Salads are an integral part of Western dining experience. Raw vegetables like lettuce, tomatoes, carrots, and celery are staple foods of a Western diet. Americans often eat salad as a healthy lunch.

But, to Chinese diners, eating raw vegetables is the opposite of healthy; raw vegetables are seen as dirty and unsafe to eat. Cooking them, either by steaming, stir-frying or boiling (depending on the vegetable), makes them soft, hot and moist... which, for the Chinese, is healthy and refreshing!

Therefore salads in China are only available at Western restaurants because nearly all Chinese consumers favor cooked vegetables.

53. Please Take Away the Heads

First-time visitors to China never fail to be shocked when they order a poultry dish and the chicken or duck head comes out on the plate, often staring right at

their face when the plate is respectfully placed in front of them. For Americans who have never even seen a dead chicken head in grocery stores, let alone on a dinner plate, it can be unsettling.

For the Chinese, however, when they order a whole roasted duck, they want to see the whole duck on the dinner table. If the restaurant served it without the head or the feet, the customer would think that the kitchen staff had eaten part of the duck. Similarly, when you order seafood in China, the kitchen staff will come out with a fish or a lobster still flopping and struggling in a black plastic bag to show you that it is indeed fresh and alive. My friends and I always joked that we should mark the fish with a permanent marker just to make sure that the staff doesn't switch it for a different one in the kitchen.

Sometimes the heads are more than displays on a plate. They are considered delicacies in their own right. The duck tongue and the duck brains, for example, are popular among Chinese diners.

So if you don't want to see the head of your dinner fowl staring at you from your plate, you should request that the wait staff not to bring out the heads when you order your Peking Duck.

54. The Ways of Water

At a Western restaurant, the first question the waiter asks is what kind of water you want to drink: bottled or tap, with gas or without. At a Chinese restaurant, the first question is what type of tea you want to drink. You would never be offered water, because the Chinese consider it unhealthy to drink water during meals.

During dinner at a local Chinese restaurant, one of our friends finally asked the waiter why the Chinese will drink tea and soup at dinner, but won't drink water. The waiter explained that tea is good for cleansing your mouth between bites, and that soup is healthy and tasty. However, he said, drinking water will dilute the stomach's digestive acids, making it more difficult to digest the meal and leading to indigestion.

Americans and Chinese also have different views on drinking cold water and other drinks. Most Americans like their drinks cold, preferably with ice cubes, and don't like to drink room temperature water. Most Chinese, however, drink room temperature or warmer liquids, like tea, and avoid cold drinks and ice. They feel that the cold temperature is a shock for one's stomach and internal organs, and that warm fluids are healthier for the body.

55. Rice or Noodle

Different cultures also have different expectations regarding food and drink. No one is surprised to hear that a Western person expects to be offered coffee at a meeting, whereas a Chinese person expects to be offered tea. But on airlines, the differences in expectations are more surprising.

On Western airlines, when flight attendants offer a choice of entrées, it is typically a choice of protein: "Would you like beef or chicken?" But on Chinese airlines, they offer you a choice of carbohydrates: "Would you like rice or noodles?" We were traveling with my in-laws on a domestic Chinese airline, and when the stewardess asked us whether we wanted noodles or rice, my father-in-law asked what meat choices came with the set—beef, chicken, pork, or fish? The stewardess was puzzled. She didn't actually know, and didn't think it was a relevant question! (It turned out that both noodles and rice came with pork, a staple food in Chinese diet.)

A common myth in China is that Westerners are stronger, less afraid of cold weather, and hardier because they grow up eating steaks and cheese. Conversely, Chinese are less strong because they grow up on rice and gruel!

56. Noodles for Birthdays

In the West, cakes are a must for birthday parties. In China, while the cake is optional, noodles are a must.

Because noodles are long, they symbolize long life. The Chinese believe that if the birthday person eats noodles on this special day, he will enjoy a long life ahead. This is why birthday noodles are often not cut. They are stretched from a single piece of dough into long strings of skinny noodles. When you eat the noodles, you should try not

to cut them with your chopsticks either. Only when you can't stuff any more noodles into your mouth, can you bite them off.

In big cities in China today, many people will celebrate birthdays with both birthday cake and noodles. While cakes are enjoyed by friends and family members attending someone's birthday, noodles can be eaten by those who are absent from the actual party. On my side of the family, we will eat noodles on a cousin or an aunt's birthday even if he or she lives in a different country. We hope by our eating noodles, they will live a long and healthy life.

57. The Hundred-Year-Old Egg

In southern China, the "Hundred-Year-Old Egg" is a very popular side dish for breakfast. Called *pidan*, it is a black-brown colored, hard-boiled egg with a translucent egg white, a grayish blue yolk and a distinct sulfur smell. Most Chinese like to dip the *pidan* in soy sauce and eat it with breakfast congee, or rice porridge (though I must point out that not all Chinese like pidan; my father, for one, loathes it).

Most foreigners cringe when they see this Chinese delicacy. Both the sight and the smell are so unusual that many people find it revolting. But it really can be quite delicious when cooked into the congee with minced chicken.

Bryan was first introduced to *pidan* during one of our *dim sum* meals in New York's Chinatown. I have learned not to tell him exactly what he is eating until he has at least tried a bite. After raving about how delicious the congee was, he asked me what the dark-looking pieces were. I said "Chinese mushrooms" at first, but eventually, I told him what he was eating. After close examination of the *pidan* in its original form, Bryan affectionately called it "The Hundred-Year-Old Egg." It sure looks like it has been sitting there for a hundred years!

Explanatory Notes:

Contrary to its looks, pidans are not rotten eggs that have been kept for a hundred years. They are made from fresh duck eggs (I don't know why chicken eggs are not used) wrapped in layers of mud and straw, and then placed in lye for at least a month. Apparently, the basic properties in lye 'cooks' the egg and hardens it so that the egg appears hard-boiled after the process.

58. "Stinky but Yummy"

A year ago, Bryan's big bosses came to China from overseas for a board meeting. In order to give them a proper welcome, Bryan scoured the restaurant guides and decided on a very famous and expensive Chinese restaurant.

When they arrived at the restaurant, they were all quite impressed by the beautiful antique décor of the place. Massive wooden armoires, solid tables and intricately carved chairs filled the dining rooms. But as they sat down for dinner, they noticed a slight odor, a whiff of an unpleasant smell. At first, no one said anything, but even-

tually the smell became so overpowering that everyone started to wonder aloud what was causing it.

Little did they know that the restaurant was famous for its signature dish — *stinky tofu*. Stinky tofu is tofu that is fermented, like Roquefort cheese, and is served as a massive, blackened and smelly cube. Both its unsavory color and the strong smell are indications that the tofu is "well aged" and skillfully prepared. The "stinkier" the smell, the more delicious the flavor. In fact, the smell was so strong at the restaurant that it had seeped into the antique furniture, and even the beautiful armoires had taken on the stinky tofu aroma.

But for Bryan and his overseas bosses, the smell nearly spoiled an otherwise pleasant dinner. Much of the dinner conversation turned into making fun of the smelly experience. The bosses even joked with Bryan that it may be career-limiting to subject their noses to such abuse. But when asked whether they would go back to that restaurant again, they said, "Absolutely, the food was delicious. We will just bring a stack of air fresheners along. Maybe we could even sell them for a profit at the door!"

While Chinese people do not mind the smell of stinky tofu, they often do not like the smell of European cheeses. Many years ago a Chinese businessman traveled to France, and he was invited by his French business partner to a fabulous dinner. At the end of the meal, the host ordered a large plate of expensive cheeses for his guest. Among them were a few types of blue cheese complete with moldy spots and rancid odor. The Chinese businessman took one whiff of the cheese and had to suppress his gag reflex. He shook his head and asked me, "How could they eat that stuff? It smells just like dirty socks!"

59. Jellyfish, Sea Cucumbers, and Goose Feet

Many foreigners, when invited to a Chinese banquet, will say out of politeness that they eat everything. But I often find that non-Asians really have trouble with jellyfish, sea cucumbers, and goose feet (amongst many other body parts and internal organs which tend to be offered). But in China, these are signature dishes in a banquet for honored guests. In particular, sea cucumbers and goose feet in abalone sauce are some of the most expensive items on a Chinese menu.

Many Westerners find the consistency of jellyfish and sea cucumbers unpalatable. Jellyfish has been described as plastic and sea cucumbers akin to slugs. And goose feet, well, most Westerners have a hard time choking them down (Bryan being one of them). The Chinese, on the other hand, prize them because jellyfish lowers cholesterol, sea cucumbers are thought to be the best form of protein on earth, and goose feet provide collagen that helps prevent wrinkles.

If your host orders these expensive entrées on your behalf and you don't touch them (they are often served in individual portions), then you may inadvertently offend your host. The better way to handle it is to tell your host ahead of time that you don't like these types of food. Alternatively, say what you

119

WOULD like to eat, such as Peking duck, or stir-fried chicken with chili peppers. If your host insists on ordering jellyfish, sea cucumbers or goose feet, you can politely offer them to anyone else who might like them at the table. Your host won't be offended as long as the food does not go to waste.

60. A Tofu Meal for the Funeral

The word "*tofu*" has a several secondary meanings in Chinese. It doesn't just refer to food.

"Eating a tofu meal," for example, is actually a special term for the meal a family eats after a funeral. Chinese culture is heavily influenced by Buddhist beliefs. Many Chinese believe that, at least for the day of funeral, the entire family and close friends who are invited to this special meal should eat vegetarian foods. A tofu dish is central to the meal, and is served either as a stir-fried tofu with green vegetables and mushrooms,

or as a plain tofu soup with a few leaves of bok-choy. Additionally, the color white symbolizes death in Chinese tradition, so the meal's white color is another important factor.

Recently, however, more and more Chinese are adding non-vegetarian items into the menu to please their guests. Restaurants are happy to provide meats because it enhances both the quality and cost of this special meal. Further, making the meal more extravagant is seen as expressing the family's deep gratitude towards friends who gave flowers and money for the funeral.

VII
Shopping and Gift-giving

61. The Art of Bargaining

Bargaining at markets is part of the shopping ritual. Vendors expect it from the customers, and customers know that they must do it.

When we first arrived, I found this endless bargaining tedious. From buying vegetables to shopping for a pair of sunglasses, I spent hours haggling with the vendors. Part of the problem comes from not knowing how much things should cost, so I didn't know whether the asking price was reasonable or not. Part of the problem stems from my competitive nature to "win" the bargaining battle. Eventually things were not getting done because I spent too much time haggling and I got very frustrated.

Luckily, I had help from my cool-headed husband and my shopping savvy friends. Bryan's advice was "Pay what you think is reasonable regardless of the asking price." As long as I think the price is fair in my own mind, then I don't waste time bargaining. After all, my time is also valuable. My expatriate friends also gave me their tried-and-true bargaining tips. If the vendor treats me like a foreigner, then I start by asking for a 90% discount from the asking price. Then we work up until about 1/3 of the asking price. I should walk away for dramatic effect if necessary. I found this bargaining tip to be quite helpful, especially shopping for souvenirs at the market. But with vegetable and fruit vendors, I have completely given up. The price fluctuates so much with different seasonal items that I now shop only in supermarkets where prices are not negotiable.

Explanatory Note: Not Everything Should Be Bargained For

I recently spoke to the manager of our favorite massage parlor. It is a very professional salon with talented massage therapists who can melt a stiff neck and sore shoulders into soft butter. The manager lamented that expatriates who have lived in China too long have picked up "bad" habits. "What habit?" I asked. She said they come in the shop and bargain the treatment prices with her as if they were shopping at the open markets. And they get offended when told prices are not negotiable. She felt it was quite rude and disrespectful to ask for discounts at formal business establishments.

Many boutique shops now have signs that say "No Bargaining", and they are firm about the policy. I like these shops because it makes shopping easier.

62. How Much Did You Pay for That?

Culturally, it is completely acceptable in China to ask how much you paid for things. For example, housekeepers ask how much you paid for the fruits and vegetables you just bought at the farmer's market, and drivers ask how much your new sunglasses cost at the street vendor. Inevitably, they will tell you how much you have overpaid.

Many of my non-Chinese friends find this habit annoying. First, they are not used to people asking how much they paid for things. What they buy and how much they paid for it is considered a matter of privacy. Additionally, they don't like to know that they've been cheated by the local vendors yet again.

The Chinese, I find, usually ask how much you paid for things for two reasons. First, they are curious. They always want to be up-to-date on how much things cost. Second, and perhaps more importantly, they care about you and don't want you to be taken advantage of by vendors. For example, some of my friends' drivers volunteered to bargain for them at the markets so that they get a better deal. And my housekeeper is genuinely happy for me if I got a good deal on a purchase. Despite their Chinese employee's good intentions, many Westerners still find it uncomfortable to be asked how much they paid for things.

After living in China for a few years, my expatriate friends have learned how to deal with this cultural difference. To strangers who are curious, my friends just tell them to mind their own business. To people who genuinely care, they typically decide to tell "little white lies." They often tell their drivers they got a lower price than what they actually paid so that the drivers would think they got a good deal and wouldn't worry about them.

63. Loyalty Matters

Although it is a well-known fact that vendors in Shanghai tend to take advantage of foreign shoppers by charging them higher prices, they do give preferential treatment to returning customers.

I met an American flight attendant on my way back to Shanghai. She told me that she flies to either Beijing or Shanghai twice a month. And she just loves coming to Shanghai. She loves the food, the shopping, but best of all, the relationships she has made here.

When she first came to Shanghai, she was charged high prices at the pearl market. But later, as she and her fellow flight attendants returned to buy from the same vendors, they received excellent prices for their goods. Now all the flight attendants go to those shops because they know they will get quality products at low prices without having to bargain. In return, the flight attendants recommend the vendors to other travelers which works well for the vendors. They have become more like friends to each other.

In fact, when occasionally the flight attendant didn't bring enough money with her, a vendor would offer to let her pay the next time she came to China.

Often vendors would even deliver custom-made pearl necklaces to the flight attendant's hotel to save her time and hassle. The flight attendant was so amazed by the quality of the service that she said to me, "Can you ever imagine that happening at home in the United States?"

Customer loyalty is very much appreciated in China, especially in Shanghai. Most of my expatriate friends keep a big rolodex of business cards from various vendors. We all have our favorite shops and vendors where we buy our clothes, shoes, and jewelry. Becoming friends with the vendors not only saves money, but also saves the time that would have been spent on haggling!

64. Lucky Coin

Have you ever noticed a coin taped on a shop vendor's calculator in China? When I first saw that, I thought maybe the calculator was broken, and the vendor had to tape a coin on it to hold something in place. But a friend later explained to me that the vendor put it there intentionally to bring good luck. Coins represent money, and the vendor taped one on her calculator to bring more business to her shop every time she uses it.

Chinese people also use coins in other ways to bring good fortune. In Shanghai, when people renovate their apart-ments, they put a coin in the foundation before they

lay the floor to bring wealth to the household.

In Northern China, a few new, clean coins are randomly put into dumplings during the Chinese New Year. When the family enjoys the festive dumpling meal together, the persons who get the coin-filled dumplings will have a prosperous year ahead.

Bryan tells me that hiding coins in food is not unique to China, because when he was growing up in Colorado, his mom used to wrap coins and paper clips in individual aluminum foil packets and hide them in her home-baked birthday cakes. He would feel very happy to get a quarter in his piece of cake, and would be disappointed if he only got the paper clip!

65. Don't Open Gifts in Front of Others

Gift-giving is a staple of Chinese culture. Nearly every festival celebration, important business meeting and family event involves some exchange of gifts. However, unlike in some Western countries, Chinese gifts should be opened in private, not in front of the gift-giver.

For example, I recently gave a Chinese friend of mine a painting, but she didn't open it until after she got home. Bryan found this hard to understand, because he is used to people opening up gifts in front of him, so he can see their expression and tell if they like the gift right away. "It's funny," he said, "that you have to wait for them to text message you to tell you that they like your gift, rather than have them open it right away and tell you personally."

From the Chinese perspective, however, people should avoid seeming too eager to receive gifts, and this is why they should refrain from opening gifts in front of others. If someone too eager to get gifts, they are perceived as greedy, whereas someone who modestly puts the unopened gift aside for later is deemed more cultured.

66. "Special Treatment" of Foreigners

Foreigners living in China are perceived to be wealthy by the average Chinese. The Chinese believe that foreigners have the money to buy luxury goods, so therefore they should. In fact, our *ayis* (nannies) at home think Bryan should buy a Mercedes to drive to work. One of them said, "That would be a piece of cake for you." By the same token, the Chinese believe that since the foreigners have money, they should pay more than the Chinese do for things they purchase. They believe that this is only fair. So from market vendors to tailors, merchants all "jack up"prices for *laowai*.

For example, our *ayi* took Bryan's broken shoe to the cobbler to be re-paired. He took one look at the gigantic size of the shoe (Bryan wears a size 46) and said,"Isn't this a foreigner's shoe? He must have plenty of money, so just throw that away and tell him to buy a new pair." To that, our witty *ayi* replied,"Yeah, he threw it away, but I want it for my son. So please give me a good price and fix it!" Once it was fixed, she gave it back to Bryan. She told the cobbler the story in order to save money for us. In her eyes, we are not just foreigners anymore. We are family to her now, so she does everything possible to protect us!

67. Food, Alcohol, and Cigarettes as Gifts

In China, building a network is absolutely crucial for any kind of business success. Gift giving and gift exchanging is a key component in the building of networks. Unlike in the West, Chinese don't typically give chocolates, red wine, or flowers for gifts. Specialty food, hard alcohol, and cigarettes are the Chinese's gifts of choice to someone from whom a favor is needed.

By food, I don't mean home-baked cakes or cookies. Instead, I am talking about expensive delicacies that are regional and seasonal specific. For example, the fall is the hairy crab season in China. Since these crabs are only in season for a short time and are only produced in the area near Shanghai, they are a prized delicacy. Most people in China enjoy eating hairy crabs. Therefore, large and expensive hairy crabs make an ideal gift for an important person.

Another popular food gift during the mid-autumn festival is moon cakes. Mid-autumn festival occurs once a year on August 15th of the lunar calendar. So it usually falls somewhere in mid to late September on the solar calendar. It is traditionally a family holiday, similar to the American Thanksgiving, where everyone gets together for a family meal. In recent years, the mid-autumn festival has evolved into more of a commercial holiday where everyone exchanges moon cakes.

Moon cakes are round pastries that have a variety of fillings. Traditionally, they are sweet with lotus seed paste or red bean paste as fillings. These days, restaurants and bakeries make moon cakes to suit everyone's taste buds. You can buy salty Peking duck-filled moon cakes as well as ice-cream filled ones. They also make moon cakes that fit everyone's budget and gift-giving needs.

The cheapest ones cost less than one US dollar apiece. But the expensive ones which might contain shark fin, birds' nest or abalone fillings can cost over several thousand US dollars per box. I was told some boxes are made of gold while others might contain a pair of ivory chopsticks.

While crabs and moon cakes are gifts suitable for everyone, expensive liquors and cigarettes are the typically gifts for Chinese men.

Unlike their Western counterparts who like to give bottles of red or white wine as gifts, the Chinese prefer hard liquors. In rural areas and small to medium-sized Chinese cities, people like to give Chinese-made grain alcohol or *baijiu* as gifts. The most famous brands are *Wuliangye* and *Maotai*. Similar to vodkas, these *baijiu* are very potent and contain 40% alcohol by volume.

Imported liquors in beautiful bottles also make excellent gifts in China. Remy Martin, Martell, Johnny Walker, Chivas and XO Cognacs are the most frequently preferred brands for gift exchange. Interestingly, the Chinese typically don't drink them. They tend to either put the bottle in a prominent display case or pass it on to others as a gift. I've often asked people why they don't drink the liquor. Most often people say that it is too expensive and too pretty a gift to consume. Putting a nice bottle of liquor on display shows friends and family that they are financially well-off and can afford expensive imported liquors.

Like liquors, cigarettes are also popular gifts for Chinese men. Most men in China smoke. In fact, in northern China there is a saying, "You are not a man if you don't smoke." But there are specific etiquette to follow when giving cigarette gifts.

First, the brand matters. The Chinese will give expensive brands for important occasions, and much less expensive ones for small matters. For example, the most popular cigarette for gift purposes is called *Zhonghua*, or China. It is a fairly expensive brand, ranging from $50 to almost $300 per carton. It is THE cigarette to give if you need to ask someone for a big favor. The Chinese say that "People who buy *Zhonghua* don't smoke it; people who smoke *Zhonghua* don't buy it." In other words, people who buy it cannot afford to smoke it themselves, but people who smoke it don't need to buy it themselves because they are so powerful that they always receive *Zhonghua* as gifts.

Second, when you give cigarettes, you must give two cartons of them. The Chinese believe even numbers are more auspicious, therefore it is good luck to give a pair of cigarette cartons as gifts. If you only give one carton, people will think that you are miserly and insincere.

In recent years, people are becoming more health conscious. In big cities, some people have become more hesitant about giving cigarettes as gifts. In order to mollify the negative effects of cigarettes, some will give a couple boxes of ginseng with the cigarettes. They hope that, this way, the healthy ginseng will cancel out the unhealthy cigarettes!

68. Red Envelopes

In China, most gifts for Chinese New Year, weddings, tips, and so forth, are cash rather than actual items. People put the money inside little red envelopes, called *"hong bao."*

People give money for practical purposes: the recipients can buy what they want as opposed to receiving gifts that they may not want.

Most Chinese stores do not have gift certificates, nor return policies, so giving cash ensures the recipient gets something that they like and don't already have.

For weddings, people give money because there is no tradition of a gift registry and people can use this money to get started as a couple.

Parents give their child a *hong bao* for Chinese New Year. They always give brand new, crisp bills because children must wear all new clothes on New Year's Day and everything they hold should signify a clean start to the year. Children even have a song they sing that goes *"gong xi fa cai, hong bao na lai"* which literally means, "Happy New Year, please give me my red envelope!"

69. Never Give a Clock as a Gift

When we moved to Shanghai, we met a wonderful couple from Texas. They have a great Chinese driver whose only fault was that he tended to over-sleep in the mornings. Our friends found out that he didn't have an alarm clock and decided to buy him one so that he wouldn't be late in the future.

Fortunately, our friends spoke to their Chinese secretary about the matter prior to giving their driver a clock. They learned that according to Chinese custom, it is taboo to give someone a clock as a gift. The word clock is "*zhong*", which sounds exactly like the word for funeral. Thus, giving someone a clock, or "*song zhong*" in Chinese, sounds exactly like the phrase "attending someone's funeral." Due to this similarity, a Chinese person would never give another Chinese person a clock as a gift.

As a result, our American friends spoke to their Chinese driver before giving him the alarm clock they got for him. They explained that the clock was not a gift to him, but was rather a work necessity. Their driver was not offended by the gesture. Instead, he appreciated their thoughtfulness and became more punctual.

VIII
Understanding the Chinese Family

70. Living with Parents

When Western people graduate from college and/or get their first jobs, they typically move out of their parents' house and live independently. In the United States, for example, it is generally a social stigma to continue living with one's parents after reaching adulthood.

In China, however, most young people will live with their parents until they get married. Many couples will even continue to live with one set of parents after marriage. When the young couple has a child, at least one pair of grandparents will live with them or very close so that they can help them raise the child.

Unlike their European or American counterparts, a young Chinese person is rarely financially independent from his family. Many young people, upon graduation from school or university, will give a portion of their salary to their parents. Thus they contribute to the household income since their parents are paying for housing, utility and food bills. Some will turn over their entire salary to their parents and will receive an allowance back for personal spending.

The parents, in return, must save enough money to pay for their child's wedding gift. For sons, they are obligated to buy an apartment when he gets married; and for daughters, many will buy a car for the new couple. This is why many couples in large Chinese cities like Shanghai prefer to have daughters rather than sons, because the financial burden of having a son is much greater (in rural areas of China, there is still a strong preference for sons). Furthermore, they will be expected to raise their grandchildren, because nearly all Chinese women will return to work full time after the baby is born. As the parents grow older, the young couple is expected to take care of them in their old age.

When Chinese families move abroad, many of them still retain this close-knit family relationship and help their children financially. Among well-established immigrants, parents often buy their children their first house, so that they will not be burdened with mortgage payments. In return, the parents can visit their children whenever they want to, and can stay for months at a time. If a young couple is living abroad when they have a child, and their parents are still living in China, they will typically either send the child back to China for the grandparents parents to raise, or would ask the grandparents to come abroad to take care of the baby.

71. Love through Food

When Chinese people like you, they often show their affection by feeding you. This certainly was how my parents and relatives welcomed Bryan into our family.

The first year we were married, we went to my parents' house for Thanksgiving. My mother spent two whole days preparing the meal. The night before Thanksgiving, we could hear her pounding the pork chops well after midnight. The next day, we had an absolute feast. Bryan's plate was piled high with all kinds of food. Throughout the dinner, my mom would goad Bryan to have more of

this or that, and would keep refilling his plate with more and more food. Since it is rude not to clean your plate at a Chinese family meal, Bryan had to finish every single bite on his plate to be a good son-in-law. At the end of the meal, he was literally begging my mom not to serve him any more.

Similarly, whenever we visited our relatives in China, they would always ply him with enormous amounts of food. Bryan joked, "No wonder I am always getting heavier. Your family is always stuffing me with food! So tell them they can't say that I've gotten fatter every time they see me. It's all their fault!"

Cultural Comparison:

My husband's family members show their affections to me very differently. The first day I met Bryan's mom, we knew we really liked each other. Nevertheless I was unprepared when she gave me a big hug. That's when I knew she really liked me! Bryan's dad, on the other hand, took me on a snow shoeing trip in Colorado the first time I met him. When we reached a lake covered in deep snow, he picked me up without warning and threw me in the snow. As I landed on my back, he smiled and said, Now you can make a proper snow angel! And my brother-in-law showed his approval of me by throwing a snowball at me while I was trying to take a picture of him and Bryan. The snowball landed square in my camera lens. I was so surprised that I fell backwards into the snow, again! This was how I was welcomed into his family!

72. "You Gained Weight!"

When I was growing up, every time I came to China to visit my extended family, the first thing they would comment on was my weight. And usually, it was "You've put on more weight!"

After Bryan and I got married, he became the primary target for "weight watch." Even though his weight had barely changed, people would still comment on his weight before even saying "hello." Bryan was annoyed at these "rude" comments. "Why are they so obsessed with my weight?" He would complain.

Many of my expatriate friends also had the same problem. A few ladies complained that when they return to China from their summer vacations back home, their Chinese housekeepers would greet them with "You've gotten fat!" Even if it were true, it was still upsetting to hear it.

The Chinese, however, often say that to show their affection. It indicates their familiarity with you. It is almost their way of saying, "Hey, long time no see. I've missed you." By noticing your minute weight changes, they are saying that they care about you enough to notice the difference.

In recent years, however, I observed that young people in China are more tactful about saying someone is getting fat. Body image has become more important among young Chinese. In fact, everywhere I look, I see advertisements for diet programs and body slimming treatments. My Western friends often attribute the slender figure of Chinese women to skinny genes, but little do they know that almost all the Chinese women I know are on some sort of diet to keep their weight down. Thus calling a friend "fat" would now come across as insulting.

73. Money and Family

Many of our Chinese friends don't understand the relationship between Western parents and their children regarding money. They find it hard to imagine that Western parents can just watch their children struggle to make a living when they themselves have a lot of money. Our Chinese friends have often asked us why Westerners are like this, and why parents don't just give their children some money. We explain that most Western parents do help their children if

it becomes necessary, but that most of the time they hope their children will be independent and not rely upon their parents for financial assistance.

In China, however, many parents don't want their teen children to take on internships or work in the summer. They think it is too much of a hardship for their kids. And socially, they think only poorer families send their children to work for money. Therefore, it is not socially acceptable for Chinese children to work at summer jobs if their family can afford otherwise. That is why many college graduates in China have much less work experience than their Western counterparts.

74. Wife Walks behind Husband

When Bryan's parents came to China for visits, the four of us would often take walks around our neighborhood after dinner. Our Chinese neighbors would often comment on how romantic Western people are, because even though they are already in their sixties, my in-laws still hold each other's hands when they walk.

In China, you would rarely see couples over forty years old hold hands when they walk together. In fact, most couples stop holding hands after they are married, especially after having children. When the child is small, one parent would be holding the child. When the child can walk, he or she would walk in the middle of the parents. When the child reaches teenage years, a boy would walk close to the mother and a girl would hold hands with the mother, but both would walk behind the father.

Among older couples, you will almost always see the wife walking a few steps behind the husband. Perhaps they will walk side by side if they are engaged in a conversation, but as soon as the conversation stops, they will automatically revert to a staggered formation. When they go out with other couples, the men will walk together and the women will walk arm in arm behind the men.

One Chinese friend observed that if you see a Chinese woman walking slightly behind a Chinese man, then you can be sure that they are husband and wife. But if you see a couple over forty years old holding hands, then you know they are either lovers having an extra-marital affair or they are dating. Our friend stressed that it is not "normal" for older and married Chinese couples to display their affection publicly.

Similarly, our friend pointed out to us that older Chinese couples do not go on "dates." While they would go to restaurants to enjoy a meal together, you would not see them in a more romantic place such as a coffee shop or a bar. Anniversaries are almost never celebrated unless it is the 40th or the 50th. And those special occasions are typically entire family or even community affairs, not a celebration just between two people. I remember when my grandparents reached their 50th anniversary, the local community officials invited them to a party for all the couples in the neighborhood celebrating their golden anniversaries. The community center even hired makeup artists, rented wedding gowns and tuxedos, and took professional portraits of all the couples. Rather than a romantic dinner for two, it was a huge community celebration.

Now that we have two children, Bryan and I have much less time to go out on our own. But we still make time for our weekly dates. On our date nights, Bryan sometimes likes to wrap his arm around me. I would often feel self-conscious when he did that. After all, we are now an "old and married" couple according to Chinese tradition. So we compromise; we just hold hands. Immediately, we are mistaken for boyfriend and girlfriend. Chinese people are always surprised to find that we have been married for nearly nine years and already have two children!

75. A Husband's Expectations

Dress Code for Wife

A good friend of mine from Shanghai was getting married. A group of us girls threw her a bachelorette party (my British friends call it Hen's Night). The dress code was "sexy." I put on a black mini dress with high heeled boots and wore bright red lipstick. Before I left for the party, Bryan said to me, "You look great, honey! Have a good time tonight."

When I arrived at the party, I found that two of my other girlfriends, both married to British men, were dressed quite sexily. Coincidentally, all of us were dressed in black. Our bachelorette friend arrived at the party late. This was unusual for her because she had always been a very punctual person. She was wearing a beautiful white cocktail dress with a deep V-neck and a big white bow at the waist. It was classic and lady-like, and her looks contrasted sharply from our black sexy outfits. She looked absolutely lovely. We all commented that she looked like Sarah Jessica Parker in *Sex in the City*. Meanwhile, she apologized profusely for being late and then explained to us the reason for her tardiness.

The dress she was wearing had padded bras sewn on the inside. When she put it on, her fiancé disapproved of it saying it made her breasts look too pronounced. Our friend cut off the padded bras and put the dress back on again. This time she was confident that her fiancé would not have any objections. Indeed, he was more comfortable with the new look. But when he found out she had taken out the padded bras, he said, "What? You are going to go out without a bra?" She had to assure him that there was no danger of exposing herself. This lengthy dressing process was the reason for her delay.

Most Chinese men are very protective of their wives. They dislike their wives attracting attention from other men. A married Chinese woman will typically dress in a conservative fashion to please her husband. When I go shopping with girlfriends who have Chinese husbands, they avoid buying anything that exposes the shoulders and backs. Even if they liked that style of dress, they would not buy it because they know their husbands would disapprove of it.

Long Distance Relationships OK

In China husbands are more tolerant of their wives working and living miles away. In fact, most Chinese don't think it is strange for husbands and wives to live in separate cities, provinces, or even countries. Being apart for months and years at a time is not unusual for many Chinese couples. Career development and the opportunity to make more money often have a higher priority than being together physically. While some will remain loyal to their partners despite the distance and separation, many do succumb to affairs. I've been told that MBA in China means "married but available."

76. Strong-headed Shanghai Woman

Women in Shanghai are known for their dominant role in the family. The stereotype (and usually the reality) is that they control the finances at home, make the family decisions, and often even delegate housework to their husbands.

Our nanny is certainly one of these strong Shanghai women. She is in her early fifties, retired from factory work, but still makes a good living as a nanny/housekeeper. Although she does all the chores in her own house, she also calls all the shots: from investing in the stock market to making decisions on a daily basis. She excels in her work at our house as well; even on her first day of work with us, she didn't need me to tell her what to do. Before I even opened my mouth to list all the household chores, she preempted me by saying, "I have done house work all my life. I know exactly what to do. Don't you worry. I will take care of everything." And with that, we started a beautiful relationship. I provide her with all the necessary supplies, from food ingredients to cleaning products, and she does her magic. I just need to stay out of her way!

Although dominant, the more traditional type of Shanghai women are at the same time chauvinistic. When it comes to decision-making power, they keep

it to themselves. But when it comes to material comforts, they put their hus-

bands and their sons first. This is certainly the case with our nanny at home. She

respects my decisions regarding all household affairs, but prioritizes Bryan's

preferences when she cooks. In fact, she cooks up a storm if Bryan comes home

for dinner, but if it is only her and me eating at home (the kids have separately

prepared meals), then she often says, "Come on, it's only us women. We can just

get by with some rice and pickles."

However, it does not mean that Bryan gets everything he wants from our nanny. Whenever I am not around, our nanny would ask Bryan directly what he wants for dinner. When he picks something, say "duck", she would disagree: "We just had that yesterday, so no, not that." He then says "sweet and sour pork." She says, "No, you said you want to lose weight. Sweet and sour pork is deep-fat-fried. You can't have it. You should eat fish. I am going to cook fish then." She speaks and walks very quickly. Even before Bryan could digest the information in Chinese and respond, she was already gone. So Bryan would usually shake his head and sigh, "Why does she bother to ask me then? She always does what she wants anyway!"

We affectionately call her our strong-headed *ayi*. But really she is just acting like any other Shanghai women: making the decisions!

IX
What They Say vs. What They Mean

77. I Know & I Understand

Sometimes small differences in words or phrases can have a large impact on the way people perceive each other. Bryan had a Chinese subordinate whose English was very good, but who had a habit of saying "I know" whenever Bryan spoke with him. In English, constantly saying "I know" to someone means that they are telling you something you already know, and stop wasting their time!

So finally one day, after hearing "I know" several times during a meeting, Bryan interrupted his colleague and said, "If you already know everything, then I guess we don't need to have these meetings anymore!" His colleague was quite shocked, because he didn't mean that at all—he was simply translating the common Chinese expression "*wo zhi dao*" word-for-word into English. What he meant by "I know" is actually "Ok, I understand." Once he explained that to Bryan, their meetings went much better!

Some months later, Bryan did the same thing to one of his other staff members. Bryan tries to speak as much Chinese as possible, and during his weekly meetings he would say "*wo ting de dong*"—which he thought meant "I understand"—whenever he got his colleague's point. After a few weeks, how-

ever, his colleague finally told Bryan to please stop saying this, because he was actually saying "I can comprehend what you are saying." In other words, his speaking was understandable. Bryan was accidentally offending the man by "arrogantly" saying that he could speak his own native language properly.

78. "No Problem" or Big Problem?

One phrase everyone learns in China is "*mei yo wen ti*," which means "No problem." Like many phrases in Chinese, however, the words can imply several meanings depending upon the situation. People must figure out if someone saying, "No problem" really means "No problem," or if they mean "Big problem!"

We hear *mei you wen ti* constantly—from taxi drivers who are lost, from Bryan's staff describing business situations and from workman trying to fix our kitchen stove. Sometimes, of course, it means that there is really no problem. It indicates that the person can take care of the issue easily or will really find the hotel without using a map. But often times, *mei you wen ti* actually means that there is a problem and the person will not be able to solve it, but doesn't want to admit it. No one likes to admit that they can't handle things, in any culture, but in China this can be very embarrassing and mean a loss of face (honor). So many times, people will say "No problem" just to buy themselves time before they must admit that they cannot solve the problem.

The best thing to do if someone says is to try and figure whether they mean "No problem" or "Big problem," and if they mean "Big problem," to help them solve it without losing their honor. For example, when I am riding in a taxi and the driver is clearly lost, but says "No problem" when I ask him if he knows where he is going, I will say "You know, this place is really hard to find, and I even can't find it sometimes... let's find it together on the map," or "I'll call the hotel and ask for directions for you." This way the driver doesn't lose face, and he will be much more willing to check a map. He will probably also appreciate that I properly understood his *mei you wen ti!*

79. Hearing What They Didn't Say

Chinese is often described as an indirect language, where people use subtle hints and implications rather than directly speaking what they want to say. My husband discovered how true this was during a recent business trip with his company CFO, when the two of them attended the same meeting but walked away with completely different conclusions.

Bryan has been learning Chinese for the past three years, and he recently felt that he could start to hold meetings with joint venture partners and other business colleagues without using an interpreter. His vocabulary is not bad, and he can understand a lot better than he can speak, so he figured it was worth a try. However, after his first trip without a translator, he came home and told me that he decided to use a translator again going forward.

"It wasn't a problem of understanding what they were saying," he told me, "because I actually understood most of the discussion quite well. And what they said sounded very positive, and very cooperative, so I felt that the meetings went extremely well. However, after the meeting, my CFO said that there were many problems with their 'cooperation,' and that we would have a tough time working with them in the future."

"When I asked why he felt this way, he laughed. 'Bryan,' he said, 'In Chinese, what is spoken is oftentimes not as important as what isn't spoken. To really speak Chinese well, you need to know a lot more than the vocabulary and grammar...you need to know what they should have said, but didn't!'"

80. Little & Old

In Chinese, adjectives like "little" and "old" don't always mean little and old. Sometimes they mean just the opposite. When we had our second child, our ayis nicknamed them "No. 1" and "No. 2". In Chinese, they are called *lao-da*, "the old and big one", and *lao-er*, "old number two", respectively. The *ayis*, however, are called by their surname with a prefix of "little." So Bryan thought it was quite funny that the babies in the house are called "old" and the older people are called "little".

Explanatory Note

Actually the prefix "xiao" or little is an endearing term given to people with whom you are familiar. It indicates the person is young, small in stature, or inferior in social position. The prefix "lao" or old also indicates familiarity. A person is called "lao" when he is older or more senior in position. Sometimes, however, "lao" is used humorously. For example, foreigners of European descent are called laowai, "good-old-foreigners!"

163

81. Wife & Mistress

Here is a story that says you can't always apply logic to language, especially when you try to translate word for word from one language to another.

After living six months in China, Bryan wanted to impress his friends with his new vocabulary words. When we met one of his business colleagues on the street, Bryan introduced his colleague to me in English, and then proceeded to introduce our son and me to his friend in Chinese. He pointed at our son and meant to say, "This is my little boy." But he only knew the Chinese word for son, not boy, and only the word for small, not little. But, he figured it was close enough. So in Chinese, he said, "This is my small son" which meant this is my younger son. The business colleague then asked, "Oh, where is your older son?" Then Bryan realized he had made a mistake. But he was not daunted by it.

After explaining what he really meant in English, he went on to introduce me in Chinese. He had recently learned the word *laopo*, a nickname name for wife, which loosely translates to "my woman" in English. Since the Chinese word for wife, *qizi* or *taitai*, is quite formal, he decided to try this new vocabulary out. But Bryan figured that "my woman" sounds a bit chauvinistic and not endearing enough, he added *xiao* or "little" to the word to indicate "my little woman." As soon as he said it, his colleague's face became quite puzzled, and I raised one eye-brow and asked him, "Really? Where is your big *laopo*?" in Chinese. What Bryan didn't realize was that by calling me *little laopo*, he had accidentally introduced me as his mistress! I responded by asking him where his real wife, the big laopo was. Needless to say, Bryan's colleague was very surprised by this family introduction!

82. What Does Your Hand Say?

Hand gestures differ widely from culture to culture, and one can easily say something inadvertently by assuming that Chinese hand gestures are the same as Western ones. Most travelers know not to use offensive hand gestures in other countries. But sometimes, even the innocuous ones can be funny and problematic.

Some German friends recently went to a local bar in Shanghai. The waitresses there spoke very little English, just enough to take orders for drinks. One German colleague decided to order a couple of beers for himself and his friend. In order to emphasize what he wanted, he spread his thumb and index fingers out into the shape of a handgun to indicate the number "2." In Chinese custom, however, this gesture means "8." A bit unsure of her English abilities but confident in her ability to read the emphatic hand gesture from the *laowai*, the waitress quickly brought back eight beers for our friends. After all, she probably thought the Germans can drink lots of beers! Our German friends were surprised, as they thought he had made it clear that he only wanted two. Bryan and I had a good laugh at the story.

X
Doing Business in China

83. Business Cards

In America, when you meet someone in a non-business setting, you exchange phone numbers on a piece of paper. In China, you exchange name cards. So one of the first things we did after our arrival was get our respective cards printed.

In addition, we learned that it is important to hand your business card out with BOTH hands. It is a sign of respect in Chinese custom. If you give your card to someone with just one hand, then it is a gesture of disrespect to that person. Similarly, when you receive a name card from a Chinese person, you must use both hands as well.

You also need to examine the card you just received and make some small comment about the card. The Chinese will typically comment on the location of your residence or company if they are in a good area of the city. Or they will say what they have heard about your company's latest development to show that your company is famous and that they are well-informed. Or they will say something flattering about your specific position in the company such as "Well, that must be a very big job you have there."

Likewise, they expect you to read their cards briefly and give your comments to show that you actually care enough to pay attention to who they are. Bryan has often found that aspect a bit difficult. Not knowing Chinese cities well, he usually cannot comment too much about their locations. And he doesn't want to accidentally say something offensive about their specific jobs. Sometimes, he resorts to commenting on their choice of English name as it is common and chic for many young Chinese people to adopt a Western first name.

The easiest and the safest thing to do when you have no idea who the person is or what his company does is to simply read the business card and say something like, "So, you are the [fill in the blank] at the [company name]? Great. Please tell me more about your company." Then you will be in a better position to make some intelligent small talk with that individual.

I Don't Have Money!

A foreign intern was working in China for the summer. He was bothered by beggars who typically target foreigners. They were especially problematic late at night because they gathered around the bars. He became so frustrated with them that he printed a bunch of business cards with the Chinese phrase: "wo mei qian" or "I have no money" on them. When the beggars stopped him, he would give out these "name cards" rather than explaining to each person that he had no money to give.

84. A Chop Makes It Legal

One popular souvenir for Western tourists to China is a "chop." A chop is a stamp which often has a person's name on it. It is pressed into an ink pad and used to stamp papers and envelopes. "Chops" make neat souvenirs, but in China, they are also crucial for signing contracts, approving company transactions, and managing Chinese businesses.

In most Western countries, the signature of a senior executive or company officer is sufficient to make the document legal and binding. In China, however, signatures by themselves do not make something legal; instead, the company must also "chop" all contracts, invoices, meeting minutes and any other legal documents. This way, contracts are not perceived to be an agreement between individuals—the people who sign them— but rather between companies. Each company has only one "chop" (or seal) and usually only one person is authorized to place it on documents and contracts. Obviously the person keeping the company "chop" holds a lot of power!

Chinese companies also use the company "chop" in a very practical way, which is to make sure that no pages in a multi-page contract are removed or changed once the documents have been approved. They will fan out the contract pages, and then chop the company seal on the fanned out pages so that each page has a slice of the company seal on it. Therefore, when you spread the pages out, you can quickly tell if any pages are missing or have been replaced with a new one; if nothing is amiss, you should be able to see the complete company seal on the edge of the pages; whereas if someone has inserted a new page into the contract or pulled one out, that page will not have a slice of the company seal on it.

85. The Boss Knows the Answer, Even When He or She Doesn't

Most people would agree that it is good to be the boss. However, being the boss in China has some unique characteristics to it. For example, while many Western cultures allow employees to question their bosses, or even challenge them during public meetings, Chinese employees are usually very deferential and do not voice contrary opinions. And Chinese bosses are typically expected to manage top-down and to know the right strategies and all the answers. So being the boss in China has a lot of pressure attached to it!

Bryan was aware of these differences when he started working in China, but he told me one funny story which illustrated this difference. During budget season, Bryan's finance team was preparing some detailed multi-year forecasts for various parts of the business. When Bryan asked one of his staff members to make a very complicated forecast, the staff agreed to do it, and then sat patiently in front of him. Bryan thought she didn't understand, so he repeated the request, but she said, "No, I understand what you want. But I need you to tell me what the right answer is, so that I can make the forecast correctly." When Bryan told her that he didn't know the answer, she laughed and continued to sit there waiting. So finally Bryan said, "Of course I know the answer, but I want to see how close your calculations are, and I'll tell you afterwards how well you did." With that, she returned to her desk and got to work.

Two days later, she returned with a very well-done projection, and Bryan complimented her on the analysis. She then asked "So, was I right?" Bryan had already forgotten their earlier conversation, but quickly remembered and told her "Yes, you were very close."

86. Sitting Side by Side

Say the word "meeting" to a business person, and they will usually imagine a conference room with people gathered around a table, reviewing documents and watching Powerpoint presentations. In many Chinese meetings, however, the participants are seated next to each other in comfortable chairs, with only a small table between them to hold their tea. Bryan calls this meeting style "sitting side by side," and for many Westerners, it is a very different way to conduct a business discussion.

During a recent trip to China, one of Bryan's bosses was invited to meet with a senior government official. His boss had prepared a Powerpoint presentation to introduce their company, and he planned to hand out copies of the presentation for review during the meeting. Bryan told him that, as this was his first meeting with this official, they would not meet around a conference table, but would actually have a more informal discussion sitting side by side. They would need to turn in their chairs to look at each other. Only later, once the relationship was established, would they have any meetings where they would sit across from each other around a table.

We think there are two main reasons for this meeting style and both are directly related to aspects of Chinese culture. Firstly, if people sit across from each other, it could make them feel like adversaries, whereas sitting side by side makes them feel friendlier, like colleagues. Secondly, in the Chinese seating hierarchy, the person sitting with their back to the door is considered subordinate to the person sitting with their back to the wall. So to avoid any unintentional implications, both people sit with their backs to the wall.

87. Eye Contact

Small differences in manners and customs can often lead to misunderstand-ings especially amongst co-workers from different countries that need to work together. One area that Bryan noticed is eye contact, or "looking each other in the eye."

In Western culture, eye contact is very important because it is a way to tell whether someone is being honest with you or not. If someone looks you in the eye and says something, it is probably true; whereas if someone does not look at you when they talk, it may mean that they are being evasive or untruthful.

For Chinese, on the other hand, eye contact is not necessary during a con-versation, and in fact, may be considered too direct. People do not "open their face" to everyone, and they control their emotions. Thus lack of eye contact does not say anything about their honesty or focus.

Recently, Bryan saw the misunderstanding that this cultural difference can cause. Two of his senior staff members, one Chinese and one Western, were working together to solve a problem, but they each had a different proposal. Finally they reached agreement. However, during the entire discussion, the Western staff kept trying to look his Chinese colleague in the eye, whereas the Chinese staff intentionally averted his eyes when he spoke. Afterwards, the Western staff told Bryan he was skeptical about whether his Chinese colleague would really support the proposal... and was surprised when his colleague fully supported him as he had promised. It was just a situation where a major cultural indicator of honesty for one person is not an indicator at all for the other.

88. The Last Two Minutes

Bryan has business discussions with his Chinese counterparts, joint venture partners and various officials nearly every week, and he has learned that the indirect approach defined by Chinese culture makes these discussions quite different from American ones. In particular, the time spent on "small talk" is much greater in Chinese discussions, and the really important part of most Chinese meetings occurs in the last two minutes.

During Bryan's meetings with Western colleagues there is usually very little small talk. The meetings often begin with some introductions and then the participants go right to the heart of the matter. They discuss issues very directly, clearly stake out their positions, and drive at a conclusion at the end of each discussion.

When meeting with Chinese colleagues, however, Bryan has learned that most of the meeting time is spent talking about everything but the key issues or decisions to be resolved. It is very indirect, with a lot of time spent on finding common ground and understanding on minor topics. In fact, he found that usually he did not discuss the key topic throughout the entire meeting. But then, at the very end, he would spend a very short amount of time discussing the most important issue(s).

Sometimes his Western bosses would get impatient because they would think that the meeting was not very efficient and was going nowhere. But Bryan would remind them that the entire discussion was necessary in order to reach the last two minutes, but that those last two minutes were worth the time!

89. What Kind of Golf Lessons Do You Want?

My husband is a golf fanatic. Thus I decided to learn golf as well when I arrived in Shanghai so that we could play together, and because the beautiful golf courses provide such a respite from city life. After buying my clubs at a golf shop, I asked the owner if he could recommend a coach to me. He asked me, "What kind of golf lessons do you want to take? You want to learn business golf or fun competitive golf?" I was perplexed by his question. I asked, "Isn't golf the same, whether you play it for business or for fun?" "No, no, no," he said. "There is a huge difference between the two."

"If you want to play business golf," he explained, "you need a teacher to teach you accuracy. You need to learn how to control the ball so that you can hit left or right as you wish. This way, when you play with a potential client or business partner, you can hit your ball in the same general area as he or she does. It provides you an opportunity to walk with the person and discuss business matters casually. On the other hand, if you want to play fun or competitive golf, then you need a coach who can teach you to hit further. Direction in this case is secondary to distance. Of course," he added, "to be a really good golfer, you would need both distance and directional control. But for beginners, you can achieve your goals much quicker if you know what kind of golfer you want to be."

I know in America, many business deals are made on the golf course. But I never thought I had to decide which strategy I preferred and what kind of lessons I wanted, like I did in Shanghai.

90. From Embarrassment to Friendship

Shortly after we came to China, Bryan invited the heads of many Chinese publishing companies to a banquet to thank them for their support over the years. Since he was new to his post, Bryan had to toast each of the publishers individually to show his appreciation.

In a display of sincerity, he emptied his glass with each of the toast. Pretty soon, the alcohol was getting to his head. He excused himself to use the bathroom, but as he got up, he stumbled on something and fell.

He was horrified. In the United States, it would be a sure loss of face. Much to his surprise, however, the Chinese publishers loved him for that. They had never met a foreigner who drank so much to befriend them. They found him trustworthy and down-to-earth. As a result, Bryan has had a great working relationship with these publishers. His little drunken accident had turned out to be a great blessing.

XI
Raising Children in China

91. Clicking and Clapping

We have two small children and because they are mixed Chinese/American, many people like to look at them and play with them. When we were in America, we were used to friends hugging our children and pinching or kissing their cheeks. In China, however, we find that both friends and strangers will interact with our children very differently from back home.

Our Chinese friends do not touch our children's faces at all, neither pinching nor kissing them, because they think this will stimulate the children's

salivary glands and cause them to drool. It is actually impolite to show this type of affection to another person's child.

Additionally, both friends and strangers will clap their hands loudly in front of our younger child (a baby girl), and will click their tongues to get her attention. This startled me at first, and it certainly startles our baby, but they do this to see if she responds to them so they can get a hug. For my Western sensibilities, however, this actually comes across as rude because it makes me feel like they think our baby is a dog! So what is normal in one culture is rude in the other and it takes some getting used to from both sides.

92. No Time to Relax

We have two small children. One day we were talking with some Chinese friends about the pressures of the Chinese education system. I remember my own experiences as a student in China, and came to the conclusion that our classes were certainly more academically rigorous at a young age than Bryan's were in America. Bryan mentioned that the U.S. school system puts a lot of emphasis on kids taking time to play, to do sports, to do social activities and so forth. Therefore, American school children have many ways to relax during their school day, rather than focusing completely on their academic studies.

When our Chinese friends heard this, they sighed and said, "Of course American children can relax; there are a lot fewer American children for them to compete with! Our children's situation is so competitive that they have no time to relax!"

93. No Crying Babies

From neighbors to elderly ladies in the street, everyone in China seems obsessed with not letting a child cry. At meal time, they tell me, you shouldn't let him cry because crying will hurt his digestive systems. Right after a meal, they tell me, you shouldn't let him cry because he will throw up. Before sleep time, you shouldn't let him cry because he will have nightmares. As you can imagine, disciplining our children is very difficult in China, because the grandparents and nannies would rather give in to our children's unreasonable demands than letting them cry.

Our son thus quickly learned that crying was his best weapon for getting his way. Unfortunately for him, Bryan and I were determined to hold our ground as parents, even if it meant letting our son cry.

A few weeks ago, Bryan took Landon, our son, to a train store to watch the electric trains go around on the tracks. Before entering the store, they made a pact that they were only there to watch and would not buy anything, since our son already had many toy trains at home. Once in the shop, however, Landon insisted that Daddy buy a train set for him. Bryan said "No." Landon started to whine; and whining quickly turned into crying. A Chinese couple in their forties came over and spoke to Landon, saying "Don't cry, don't cry. Tell your Daddy to buy you a train." Having found his supporters, Landon started crying even louder, demanding that he have a new train. Then the Chinese lady said to Bryan in Chinese, "Just buy him an inexpensive train."

Bryan got so upset that he turned to the woman and said, "He is my son. I am NOT buying him ANYTHING!" The woman scurried away. But her husband smiled at Bryan, gave him a thumbs-up, and said, "You are tough! Good for you!"

94. No Baby Showers before Birth

In America, friends and families throw baby showers for expectant mothers before they give birth. The idea is to give the expectant family gifts ahead of time so that they have plenty of time to set up the nursery before the baby arrives.

In China, it is a taboo to give baby showers before the baby's birth. In fact, it is unlucky to give expectant mothers baby gifts. Chinese people believe that a gift to the unborn might jinx the birth and jeopardize the baby's chance for survival in its early days. In Chinese tradition, which still persists today, no one except for the immediate family is allowed to see the baby and the mother for the first month after birth. After the first month, only friends and family very close to the mother can pay a visit. Extended families and other friends will not see the baby until he or she reaches 100 days. In China, the grandparents of the child will throw a large and lavish banquet to celebrate the newborn's 100th day. This is an occasion for a formal viewing of the baby. Everyone invited to the party will come bearing gifts.

The 100th day is an important milestone in a child's life. This is because it signifies that the baby has lived past the first three months during which infant mortality rate has historically been high. Although in today's China most babies born healthy will survive past three months, it was not the case even several decades ago. So the Chinese did not want to celebrate an addition to the family until they were sure it was going to live. And this tradition has persisted to the present day.

Not only do the Chinese differ in the timing of baby showers, they also dif-

fer in the gifts that they give. In the West, baby gifts predominantly consist of clothing, blankets, toys, and nursery items. In China, although people give these types of gifts as well, they are more likely to give traditional lucky charms to the newborn.

Some examples of lucky charms are longevity locks (traditional Chinese pad locks), peanuts (still in the shell), and Chinese zodiacs made of 24k gold and hung on a piece of red silk thread. Both red thread and pure gold are believed to ward off evil. Gold is also a symbol of wealth and prosperity for the child. Locks symbolize safety. Longevity locks, like its name indicates, bring the baby a long, peaceful and secure life. Unshelled peanuts are called *"changshengguo,"* or the fruit of long life, in Chinese; therefore, giving a baby a golden peanut charm is wishing him a long, prosperous life. Finally, another popular gift for a baby is a golden charm embossed with the child's Chinese zodiac sign. For example, a child born in the year of the pig will receive a golden pig charm as a good luck gift.

In short, although a Chinese baby will not receive any gifts prior to his birth, he will be showered with gold charms when he reaches 100 days.

95. Naming a Child

When giving our children English names, we looked online at long lists of names. We considered the sound of the names, their meanings, their spelling, and tried to incorporate our favorite places into them. Like most of our friends, we wanted to pick names that other kids will not tease them about.

But when the time came to pick Chinese names for our children, we went through a completely different process. Obviously they still have to sound nice, but there are more important considerations.

According to Chinese tradition, a good name must supplement and complement a person's fortune. In Chinese fortune telling, there are five natural elements that govern a person's fortune: gold, wood, water, fire and earth. A life will be good if these elements are balanced. When a child is born, his birth year, month, day and hour will combine to give him eight characters, each representing a particular natural element. If all five elements are present in a child's eight characters, then the child will be more likely to live a balanced and harmonious life. But most of the time, a person's eight characters will be unbalanced. One would have abundance in one element but a deficiency in others. (In fact, some couples will purposefully schedule a caesarean section for their baby in order to secure a balanced five elements or eight characters for their child.)

This is where the proper naming of a child becomes paramount. A good name can make up for the deficiency in elements. For example, if one is lacking water, then having a name that contains water can solve that problem. However, picking the specific name is a job for the fortune telling experts. In addition to finding Chinese characters for a name that contain the right elements, one has to also note the number of strokes in the name. The number of strokes has to fit with one's elements. Otherwise, it would adversely affect one's fortune.

After we moved to China, I sought the advice of fortune tellers to select the proper Chinese names for our children. The amazing thing was, based on our children's eight characters, the fortune tellers were able to describe my children's personalities to me. Without ever seeing our children, their descriptions matched the reality quite accurately. Although I don't blindly believe in everything the fortune teller says, I still think there is merit in this ancient art. So I worked with a fortune teller to pick Chinese names for our children in the hopes that they will have a more balanced disposition in life (and good fortune).

XII
Health and Medicine

96. Voodoo Medicine or Miracle Drug

Before coming to China, Bryan was, at best, skeptical of Chinese traditional medicine. All the talks about the "hot" and "cold" properties of food, and all the concoctions of herbal soups all seemed like voodoo medicine to him.

His opinion on the subject, however, started to change after the successful treatment of my back pain by a traditional Chinese doctor. I had injured my back early in life while in intensive dance training as a young girl. The problem worsened after I had my first baby. The physical demands of pregnancy, delivery, and improper posture during breastfeeding really took a toll on my back. Despite physical therapy, chiropractic treatment, and steroid shots, the problem persisted. In fact, it got to be so bad that I couldn't put on a pair of pants without wincing.

When I arrived in Shanghai, a family friend referred me to an old traditional Chinese doctor. He saw patients in his small apartment. He used a combination of *qigong* and homemade herbal patches to treat his patients. The herbal mixture is made from a secret recipe containing more than twenty ingredients. The ingredients are ground and then cooked into a thick black paste. It was this com-

pound that was spread onto an adhesive bandage patch. I would place patches on the areas where I had pain. I wore them for a week at a time without taking them off or getting them wet. In the meantime, I had to stay away from all raw vegetables and fruits and avoid anything sour. After four weeks of treatment, the pain was completely gone. I didn't even hurt when I went skiing for an entire week immediately after the treatment. Much to my amazement, my back pain has not returned.

My son has had a similarly good experience with traditional Chinese medicine. When he first started preschool, he was sick twice a month on average. His colds lasted so long that he seemed to have a perpetual cough and an unending runny nose. The repeated upper respiratory infections were starting to cause ear infections that were affecting his hearing. We were very worried when the ENT doctor told us that he might need surgery on his nose. Fortunately a Chinese friend introduced us to a Chinese traditional doctor who specializes in pediatrics. After a few weeks of treatment, our little boy became much healthier. Both his nose and ear problems went away, and he now rarely gets a cold. We used to suspect he had exercise induced asthma because he would cough as soon as he started running around. Now he can run around for an hour straight without a single cough!

Both my son's and my experiences really changed Bryan's attitude toward Chinese traditional medicine. Much to my surprise, he even agreed to see one himself to treat his asthma. The air pollution in China combined with his hectic travel schedule had made him quite susceptible to pulmonary problems. But after he saw our son's doctor (who kindly agreed to take on an adult patient), Bryan's immune system seemed much more resilient to viruses. Now he is definitely a believer in this ancient art. Even the terrible tasting herbal drinks didn't seem so bad to him anymore. He would take his herbal drink everyday at 10am and 3pm. In our house, we call our traditional Chinese doctors the miracle workers!

97. The Importance of Wearing Socks

Our son, Landon, was born in New York City in the middle of an extremely cold winter. He became resilient to cold weather as a result. When the following spring arrived, he stopped wearing socks with his shoes or sandals. It was September when we moved to China and the weather was still quite hot. I took him to a park near our apartment. Along the way, several older ladies stopped me to say, "How can you leave the house without putting socks on him? He is going to catch cold." At first, I tried to explain to them that he is not cold and that he is used to not wearing socks. But after the first couple of ladies spoke to me, I started to get annoyed. I wanted to tell them to mind their own business, but I didn't want to be too rude or confrontational. So I pretended I couldn't understand them. I was literally interrupted at every block. After a few trips to the park, I got so frustrated and annoyed by the constant nagging that I finally gave in and bought a few pairs of socks for him to wear.

Later I noticed that most Chinese women, especially those over the age of forty, wear socks all year round. In the summer, you will find older Chinese women wear ankle-length nude socks with their sandals. The younger and more fashion conscious ones often wear pantyhose even on the hottest summer days. And others would wear knee-high nylons with their skirts. The look was pretty horrible from a fashion standpoint, but more importantly, how could they stand wearing socks in the heat and humidity?

A few months later, a family friend explained to us the virtue of wearing socks all year round. Many older Chinese believe that it is crucial to keep the feet warm, especially in the middle of the summer heat. The sweat glands are concentrated in the feet. When the body is hot, the pores in the feet are open to ventilate. That is when cold air is most likely to enter the body through the feet. If the feet are not kept warm, then one could catch a cold. The cold air trapped in the body could also give one backaches, neck and shoulder pains, or even headaches. In fact, this friend recommended that we wear socks to bed. He told us that when he started wearing socks to sleep that all his back problems went away. He was so persuasive in his arguments that both Bryan and I thought he should quit his day job to open a sock store!

Despite my initial skepticism, I did try wearing socks to bed a few times when I felt an ache in my back. I must admit that it did work for me. Now I sound like a sock advocate whenever I tell my friends who have pain problems to wear socks to bed. But my vanity will not allow me to wear socks in the summer with sandals. That is a fashion *faux pas* too terrible to commit.

98. Don't Sit on the Floor

As Americans, our family is used to sitting on the floor. We play on the floor at home, put our bags on the ground when we go to restaurants to eat, and even plunk ourselves down on the airport carpet while we wait to board the airplane. In short, we don't hesitate to sit on floors.

The Chinese have a definite aversion to sitting on the floor. Granted, the floors in China may be dirtier than those in America, but the aversion is more cultural than hygienic. Socially, only beggars and rubbish collectors sit on the ground. Most others, even if tired, would rather squat than sit on the floor.

I remember one time when Bryan and I took our son to visit

my grandmother in Shanghai. She has beautifully waxed hardwood floors in her apartment. Being used to playing on the ground, Landon promptly plopped himself down on the floor. Everyone around us shrieked. "No! Don't sit on the floor. It is dirty!" Bryan immediately responded, "It's OK. He can play on the floor." To lend our son more support, Bryan made an exaggerated gesture and sat down next to him. The two of them crawled on their hands and knees all over the apartment. When they got up, both of them had patches of wax all over their bodies. All my relatives started shaking their heads at the sight of two dirty "boys." But the two of them had a great time. Bryan smiled, "We can easily wash our clothes and take a bath to be clean again!"

Another time, Bryan took Landon to a nearby park to play. It was early fall, and the weather was absolutely beautiful. Landon loves to run on the grass, so the two of them took off their shoes and started playing on the grass. They would run on and off the grass, and chase each other all over the park. The Chinese bystanders gawked at them, a few old ladies even told Bryan not to go bare-foot because the ground was too dirty. When they got home, they were not allowed to walk in the house until their feet were wiped clean to the satisfaction of our nanny.

I often hear the Chinese comment, "*Laowai* kids are not afraid of getting dirty!"

Let Them Get Dirty!

Landon's kindergarten just hired a male PE teacher last year. Unlike the traditional female teachers, this new male teacher has many unorthodox ways of teaching physical education. During one of his demonstration classes, he asked a whole group of five-year-olds to crawl on their bellies in a race across the auditorium. At first, a few girls wouldn't do it because they didn't want to get their clothes dirty. The male teacher said to them, "Look at my pants; they are brand new, too. I paid a few hundred RMB for these Adidas training pants. But I crawl in them. Don't be afraid to dirty your clothes because they can easily be washed." The next round of the race, everyone participated.

After the demonstration class, the school principal asked the parent and teacher representatives what we thought of the new teacher. The older teacher was hesitant about his "get dirty" style. She was concerned, quite rightly, that many grandparents who are the primary caretakers of the children would not agree with his style. But a few of the parent representatives, especially those who have sons, whole-heartedly supported his teaching philosophy. We want our kids to push their limits, get dirty, and be manlier!

99. BO Is a Disease

One of the more difficult things to find when we first moved to China was deodorant. It is still only sold in shops that Westerners frequent. The vast majority of Chinese do not use deodorant. In fact, the Chinese believe that normal healthy people should not have body odor. Underarm odor is considered a disease in China. You will find ointments and creams at the pharmacy for treating and eradicating underarm smells.

In recent years, cosmetic companies have tried to sell deodorants to Chinese consumers. It took a long and hard advertising campaign to market the goods. Unlike in the West where deodorant ads focus on avoiding embarrassment, in China, the ads stress how fresh you will smell by applying it. One TV ad showed a beautiful young girl walking into a subway train. When she lifted her arm to hold the hand rail, a sweet fragrance permeated the train car. If you didn't know they were selling deodorant, you would've thought it was an ad for a new fragrance.

100. Male or Female?

When I lived in New York City, I had to look hard for a good female Obstetrician-Gynecologist. It just seems that most of them are male. But when I came to China, the opposite seems to be true. Almost all the Ob-Gyns are female. There is a clear preference among Chinese women to see a female doctor for their more private medical needs; whereas in America, most of my American friends think it is completely normal to see a male Ob-Gyn.

Our pediatrician in China, who practiced in New York City for many years and whose husband is an obstetrician, explained to me why. In the United States, Ob-Gyns go through the entire process with a patient. He monitors the patient for the whole of her pregnancy and most likely delivers the baby, too. Therefore, he keeps a very exhausting schedule: seeing patients during the day, and being on call for deliveries at all times. Often deliveries seem to be in the middle of the night. The job is extremely demanding, physically and time intensive. It is very tough for a woman who is married and has children to keep those kind of working hours. This is why American obstetricians are predominantly male.

In China, however, obstetrics and gynecology are typically separate jobs. Obstetricians, furthermore, have regular shifts. The patients don't usually know who will be delivering their babies unless they have a scheduled caesarean. The combined factors of a less demanding schedule and the Chinese women's refusal to have a male doctor see their private areas result in China's female domination in Ob-Gyn medical practice.

It is an interesting observation that Chinese and Western men also have a different preference when it comes to massage therapists' gender. Most Chinese men don't mind a male therapists working on them. Some, in fact, prefer it because the male therapists have stronger hands. But most European and American men are very uncomfortable with male masseurs. Bryan, for one, thinks it is weird to have another man touching him when he is nearly naked. The owner of a massage parlor once told me that it is good to have a massage therapist who has a different gender than you. She believes that we all need to have our *yins* and *yangs* balanced by the opposite sex. A male therapist can restore the *yang* to a woman, and vice versa for the male customer.

101. New Mother's Confinement

Our daughter was born in the same month that our son started at a local pre-school's international division in Shanghai. Although, during that month, I delegated the drop-off and pick-up duties to our nanny, I was determined not to miss any parent-teacher conferences at our son's school. The first parent-teacher conference took place when our daughter was just two weeks old. After rearranging my nursing schedule, I went to the school for the meeting. Everyone there was astonished to see me. For the Chinese, it was unthinkable for me to leave our house before the one month post-birth confinement period was up.

In fact, *zuoyuezi*, or the month-long, post-birth rituals are the most well observed and well respected rituals in Chinese tradition. *Zuoyuezi* literally means "sitting for the month" in Chinese. During this time period, a new mother is not allowed outside of her house so that she won't catch a cold from blowing wind. In addition, she is not supposed to shower or wash her hair because it might give her arthritis or chronic headaches when she gets old. Only sponge baths are allowed. She cannot hold the baby except to breast feed so that her muscles are not strained, and she must stay in bed as much as she can to avoid back problems. Furthermore, she has to follow a diet regimen. This regimen varies depending upon where she lives in China. Most diets require the drinking of a lot of chicken or fish soup without any salt added to promote the production of breast milk. In order to protect her eyesight, a new mother is not allowed to watch any television or read any books or magazines. And, to make sure she does not catch any cold air in her joints, she has to wear long-sleeved shirts, long pants and socks even on the hottest days of the summer. The ultra-traditionalists even prohibit the use of air conditioners or fans. Lastly, to help slim down her middle section, some mid-wives will wrap a ten-meter-long cotton cloth around the new mother's tummy like a shrink wrap.

While a lot of these rituals sound like medieval torture to Westerners, most Chinese women actually follow them. They believe that if they don't follow the rules, their health will suffer in their old age. My mother, for example, would often say to me that her heels hurt now because she wore slippers without socks after she gave birth to me. Another reason why the Chinese women are very strict about *zuoyuezi* is because a good monthly regimen can cure illnesses previously ailing the new mother. For example, some of my mother's friends swear that their chronic shoulder and back pains disappeared after properly observing the monthly confinement. The Chinese believe that with each birth, your body has an opportunity to reset itself. But the window of opportunity is only one month long. If you can get well rested and healthy during this month, you will enjoy a life of healthiness. But if you hurt anything during this month and do not get it fixed, you are likely to suffer the ailment all your life. This is why most Chinese women are afraid to do anything wrong during this special month.

This is also why the Chinese teachers and parents at my son's preschool berated me for violating the one month confinement. They immediately turned off the air conditioner on my account, and made sure I sat away from the fan so that no wind could blow on me. As soon as the meeting ended, they shooed me away and told me to go home. I felt like a naughty child caught breaking a curfew.

Although I tried to follow the rules, I ended up compromising on most of them. I resisted washing my hair for ten days and just couldn't stand it anymore. Just to make sure I don't catch head colds and have headaches when I get old, I made sure to blow my hair really dry. Also, I took showers every other day to stay clean and fresh. I didn't follow the rule of not holding the baby at all. She was too adorable; I just couldn't resist. As a compromise, I breast fed her while lying down to relieve any pressure on my back, and I rested a lot. I watched very little television and read less than I normally do. That part wasn't too hard since most of the time I was exhausted trying to take care of the two kids. I did follow the strict diet. Luckily for me, now you can find catering services for new mothers in China. They delivered all the food I was allowed to eat every morning. It had no salt and had a lot of soups as main entrees. The best part was that I ate nutritious food without having to worry about cooking it! One last thing, September in Shanghai was still very warm, so I did have the air conditioner going. But I adjusted the vent so that the cold air did not blow directly on me.

Comparing the two post-birth experiences, I have to admit that I felt healthier and recovered much faster by following the Chinese tradition. My back did not hurt at all where as after the birth of my son, I had really terrible back problems. The diet also seemed to help me produce more milk and lose my baby weight much faster. In fact, now I recommend this new mother's catering service to every expectant mother.

If I had another baby, I'd probably follow the Chinese *zuoyuezi* again. But my husband is convinced that two kids are quite enough for now!

Afterword

We have written a book about cultural differences between Chinese and Western people, but doing so reminds us that there are very fundamental similarities as well: We all have dreams, aspirations and desires, we all need to be loved and respected, we all want peace and stability, and we all want a better life for ourselves and our families.

The 2008 Beijing Olympic slogan of "One World, One Dream" reflects that people of different cultures have many of the same goals, just different ways of approaching them. We hope that our book has helped you to better understand how Chinese people approach their families, their traditions, their work, and each other. More importantly, we hope that it will help you appreciate their way of living, and enjoy experiencing the differences between theirs and your own.

图书在版编目（CIP）数据

如何面对中国人101题：英文／（美）沈熠，（美）
瑷秉宏著. —— 北京：五洲传播出版社，2012.12
ISBN 978-7-5085-2414-6

Ⅰ．①如… Ⅱ．①沈… ②瑷… Ⅲ．①中华文化－介
绍－英文 Ⅳ．①K203

中国版本图书馆CIP数据核字(2012)第267060号

出 版 人：荆孝敏

作   者：沈熠（美） 瑷秉宏（美）

责任编辑：王莉／朱莉莉

漫画绘制：张耀宁／刘雁峰／罗杰／庞丽

设计承制：北京画中画印刷有限公司

如何面对中国人101题

出版发行：五洲传播出版社

地 址：北京市海淀区北三环中路31号生产力大厦7层 邮 编：100088

发行电话：010-82001477 网 址：www.cicc.org.cn

开 本：710毫米×1000毫米 1/16 印 张：14

印 次：2013年2月第1版 2013年2月第1次印刷

书 号：ISBN 978-7-5085-2414-6

定 价：68.00元